D1189990

The Bamboo Principle

©Ken Lodi. Published by Network TwentyOne International, USA, 2010.

If a man has talent and cannot use it, he has failed.

If he has talent and uses only half of it, he has partly failed.

If he has talent and learns somehow to use the whole of it, he has gloriously succeeded, and won a satisfaction and a triumph few men ever know

--Thomas Wolfe

The Bamboo Principle
The Roots Beneath Results

Dedication

For those who develop their talents with steadfast enthusiasm, and valiantly strive to choreograph their efforts to discover their true potential for the greater good.

Biography

Ken Lodi is a leading authority on the subjects of Talent Optimization, Communication and Productivity. Over the past two decades, he has spoken to thousands of assembled audiences in five countries. He is the author of *Tapping Potential, Front & Center, The Bamboo Principle,* and the creator of the *Dashboard University™* audio series.

Ken is a founding partner of The Catalyst Group, a team of consultants with expertise in Workforce Development and Performance Improvement.

Table of Contents

The Foundation

I have always been fascinated by talent and peak performance, and curious about the habits and behaviors that enabled them. I didn't simply marvel at high achievers, I wanted to know more about the *roots beneath their results.* I applauded the valedictorian, but stirred in my seat, wondering how and when they studied. Today, I want to know how top athletes train; I want to know what octogenarians eat; I even slow my stride as I board my flight to notice what the passengers in first class read.

This intense curiosity was a natural catalyst to interview, research and explore great companies from aerospace to automotive, and high achievers from athletes to authors. I've identified their common practices, and drawn distinctions between occasional victories and long-term success. My "need to know more" was more than a personal quirk--I discovered it was a proven technique for self-improvement. Role models inspire confidence and clear a path for others.

The Bamboo Principle introduces the virtues shared by great companies, high achievers and Timber Bamboo—the world's strongest plant. The mission of *The Bamboo Principle* is simple and significant:

- Change the way you perceive your roles at work and home
- Learn to adapt your strengths to changing circumstances that ensure versatility
- Succeed in the broader context of *responsible achievement* and *contribution*

"Contribution" is the operative word these days as we strive to not only personally succeed, but succeed while considering our environment, social responsibility and those around us—will you live in vain or leave a legacy?

The underlying and even explicit message in this book is one of collaborative contribution. We no longer rely on the ultra-wealthy—the Gates and the Guggenheims of the world—to enable others through contribution, or, as Rockefeller put it, "the business of benevolence." Success is sweetest when you recognize your power and ability to change the lives of others for generations.

Through technology and online communities, we have democratized the joy of generosity. Philanthropy has many faces. Companies make their contributions through new technology, conscientious manufacturing and outright cash donations. We even have new career classifications such as "green-collar" workers and "philanthropreneurs." You have these opportunities as well as coaching and mentoring opportunities shared here. It's no longer only about giving money; responsible achievement and contribution include offering time, talent and expertise that—to paraphrase Lao Tzu--don't merely provide fish, they teach others how to fish.

You Want Answers

If you're like me, you've asked yourself one of the following questions:

- Am I leveraging my strengths to their full potential?
- Am I using my versatile talents on the right activities?
- Am I making the greatest contributions I can at work and at home?

If you are not happy with your answers to these questions, or truly pleased with your life-satisfaction index, then the solution often lies in the answer to the next question: "What are the secrets of those who answer a resounding yes to these questions and truly excel?"

The Bamboo Principle reveals the process and practices of great companies and high achievers who serve as our models of excellence. The development model of *The Bamboo Principle* is a useful tool and map for identifying, developing and delivering your talents consistently and in the most fertile areas. You will build your "root system" that ensures a solid foundation upon which you can expect lasting success.

People ask me about my fascination with peak performance. I answer them like Willie Sutton, the great Irish bank robber of the 1930's. When he was captured by the FBI, they asked him why he robs banks; he said, "Because that's where the money is." I study the habits and tactics of great companies and high achievers *because that's where the answers are.*

Don't study average performance unless average performance is your objective; don't study poor performance in an effort to do the opposite; it's not about what to avoid, it's about what to embrace. Model your behavior and tactics after those at the top of their game, and incorporate those ingredients in the context of your talents and value system.

In my twenty-year speaking and consulting career, I've collaborated with companies that manufactured aircraft engines, sold insurance products, assembled microprocessors, produced motion pictures, pioneered the PC, and invented life-saving pharmaceuticals. Without exception, the best at their craft employ similar business practices and create similar cultures—or *colonies*--that enable them to thrive and perform at optimum levels while feeding their talents and strengths.

What do great companies and high achievers share in common? They share the same virtues of bamboo:

- Strength
- Versatility
- Contribution

--Made possible by a personal root system that serves as the foundation for their remarkable success, and their ability to contribute responsibly to the health, convenience, and advancement of society.

Growth and success is not about outward appearances and what you *see*, it is about inward practices and what *you do*-- cultivating the proper attitudes, behaviors and strategies. This basic principle of "cause and effect" ensures the groundwork is in place for lifelong results, and that your potential isn't thwarted by shortcuts, tricks, or slipshod attempts at achievement.

Let's explore the story and significance of bamboo.

The Story and Significance of Bamboo

One lazy Sunday, I was chopping onions on my new bamboo cutting board. It still had the manufacturers tag attached that sang the praises of bamboo and bamboo products. It said a bamboo cutting board is safer than a standard maple cutting board because it is stronger, will not scar as easily from sharp knives, and therefore harbors fewer bacteria. Additionally, the various color swirls, spots, and cross-grains of bamboo provide a unique combination of light and dark textures. My cutting board soon became more conversation piece than kitchen utensil, and I began to spread the word to others.

I researched bamboo and was amazed to find that so many of the words used describe bamboo were terms you would find in books about leadership, productivity and peak performance — words like adaptive, tenacity, resilient, growth, flexible, potential, cultivate and foundation. I stumbled upon an accurate and concise analogy that represents the characteristics of what distinguishes sustainable success from short-lived victories.

How Bamboo Achieves Great Heights

When bamboo is first planted, it grows at what you would call a normal rate. After a few years, it's only a few feet tall, and remains that way until its fourth year—then it grows eighty to ninety feet in six weeks, almost two feet a day.

If you understand bamboo's potential, it's easy to wonder why your newly planted bamboo doesn't look like others in the colony. What's happening during those first few years? It is establishing a complex root system, capable of supporting its quick and impressive ascent. You require the same "foundation" before you can enjoy lasting success: how many times have you exercised and not seen immediate results? Or you read a few good business books and didn't see a change in your performance? Perhaps you've been networking or prospecting and haven't seen a spike in sales.

This is normal and often tied to laws of nature—particularly the *natural law* of reap and sow. Like bamboo, the early stages of personal growth are dedicated to foundation, not formation. Before you can experience measurable and sustainable growth, some essential skills and steps must synergize to create stability and a foundation that supports your ascent. Then, in what seems like a series of overnight results, the fruits of your efforts drop in your lap in surprising abundance. If you establish these roots—which are actually a sequence of activities--you can live the bamboo virtues of Strength, Versatility and Contribution.

Bamboo teaches that

- Growth isn't always visible
- Achievement is a process, not an event
- Success is the product of a solid foundation

These truths are represented by a simple bamboo principle: *Roots precede results*. There are no shortcuts.

It's easy to be fascinated by what appears to be quick, sudden or even overnight success. The reality is, what appears to be sudden success--or even lasting success--isn't luck; it's not just good fortune; it's the product of *deliberate efforts* and it doesn't happen overnight. There are no overnight successes, only overnight *awareness* of real talent.

We treasure the Horatio Alger stories of rags to riches, and Goethe's tales of transformation because they're inspiring, and they keep us in the game with the belief that good things can happen quickly—and sometimes they can! But when you study the histories and biographies of great companies and high achievers, you find a very different story. The road to success is often winding, fraught with perceived obstacles, and demanding of patience, persistence and perseverance. Work ethic precedes greatness.

Chapter 1

The Bamboo Principle: Roots Precede Results

"If I have ever made any valuable discoveries,
It has been owing more to patient attention
than to any other talent."
Isaac Newton

People love the notion of sudden, explosive success, but there are very few cases of overnight transformation. Your favorite rock bands, actors or investors will openly share tales of weathering failure and rejection before gaining recognition for their talents. Their success was the progressive manifestation of hard work and tenacity. They built a future, a business and a brand through consistently executing well-conceived strategies.

The Beatles "Please Please Me" reached #3 in the US in 1964, and preceded the orbital success of The Beatles performance on February 9, 1964 on the Ed Sullivan show. The media referred to this as "The British Invasion" as four kids from Liverpool suddenly emerged, taking the music scene by storm. They appeared to be gifted musicians who quickly synergized their talents and swiftly brought them to the stage and television. Nothing could be further from the truth.

John Lennon and Paul McCartney had been working intensely for almost six years prior to their big splash in the US. They played in Hamburg, Germany for several years together, performing show after show at clubs in seedy districts. After hundreds of nights of rolling, eight-hour performances, they had broadened the depth and breadth of their talents, logging twelve-hundred performances. Their sudden success was anything but sudden—it was the product of a regimented, disciplined approach to honing talents and creativity.

You can't hurry a farm, expedite a diet, or rush a retirement plan. Several factors must first synergize before you can reap what you have sown. The Great Wall of China that exists today began in the 7th century BC and was progressively repaired and renovated over several hundred years, linking old sections to new. It served a purpose in its early stages, but later showed its true potential as a barricade against invasion in the 4,000 mile-long wall that exists today.

The heights by great men reached and kept
Were not attained by sudden flight
But they, while their companions slept
Toiled ever upward through the night.

--Henry Wadsworth Longfellow

Bamboo Beans
Everybody is drinking Starbucks coffee. When I lived in New York City, I passed at least ten Starbucks' locations during the cab ride from Midtown to the Upper East Side. At the time of this writing, there are 18,000 Starbucks worldwide in forty countries. People marvel at Starbuck's explosive growth and brand presence as they bury previous brand leaders like Dunkin' Donuts,' the 1950 Boston-based company who claimed to be "the world's largest coffee and baked goods chain." Was Starbucks an overnight success? How long had their efforts been brewing before they appeared to burst on the scene with their worldwide brand?

Howard Schultz, the man who leveraged the success of the otherwise unremarkable coffee bean roaster and retailer, joined them in 1982. After traveling to Milan, Italy, and observing the charm and success of their espresso bars, he saw an opportunity to build a business and change our culture. Starbucks was soon making lattes, mochas, cappuccinos and a host of specialty coffee drinks whose accessibility today we take for granted. Ten years later, Starbucks opened a store a day and was an international brand. They are a classic example of how hard work, creativity and persistence lead to legendary, but not immediate, results. It took years to form the roots beneath their results.

You Can't Hush These Puppies

Malcolm Gladwell, author of the best-seller, *Tipping Point*, cites several examples of what appears to be explosive growth in phenomena ranging from fashion trends to crime rates. They each began as a small presence in our culture until something happened that made them tip—putting them over the top and into an epidemic of presence or popularity.

In 1958, Hush Puppies revolutionized casual footwear. The brand was immensely popular in the 1960's when Mods everywhere embraced the comfortable suede shoe. The brand then experienced a cooling period of about thirty years, until a new generation began wearing them again--not to fit in, but to stand out. Hipsters in the clubs of Soho and the East Village in New York City wore them to clubs, and they again slowly grew in popularity. Designers featured them in the window displays of their upscale boutiques. The "breeder effect" was quickly stimulated through marketing and word of mouth, and, in 1995, the Wolverine Company sold 430,000 pairs of Hush Puppies—and four times that number the following year. According to Gladwell, little things (like word of mouth) make a big difference—but not overnight. Consistent word-of-mouth "epidemics" can catapult a product into orbit with the swift progress of bamboo in its fifth year.

Unlike bamboo, you don't need to wait four years to experience quantifiable or tangible results, and you're not necessarily trying to build a business empire—but the process remains the same: there are steps and activities that must first be addressed before you can enjoy long-term growth, and the fruits of your efforts: strength, versatility and contribution.

Chapter 2

Three Bamboo Virtues: Strength, Versatility, Contribution

Great companies and high achievers model bamboos' virtues of strength, versatility and contribution through their decisions, successes, and philanthropy. These attributes ensure lasting success, renewable success, and the success of the surrounding community. These virtues are also *interdependent*.

- If you are versatile, but weak, you will not thrive
- If you are strong and versatile, but deplete your environment (financially, socially), you will not thrive
- If you are strong, contribute to your environment, but cannot adapt to changing conditions (economic shifts), you will not thrive

These virtues are the fruits of a solid foundation, and can be consciously created.

Strength
Bamboo has greater tensile strength than steel
It is twice as stable as oak, and harder than maple
It is an essential material in earthquake architecture

Strength is a personal attribute where you excel and show great potential. Strength is also a source of personal power: can you remain strong through trying times? Strength could refer to the strength of your brand or your strength as a communicator. Possessing strength in any of its forms is essential in your quest.

On April 22, 1991, a 7.6 earthquake struck Limon Province, Costa Rica, killing 53 people, injuring 198, and causing widespread damage to buildings and homes. The transportation system in Limon Province was destroyed, and many bridges collapsed. Only bamboo houses from the National Bamboo Project stood after the earthquake. Experts say bamboo has the ability to "dance" when rocked by powerful earthquakes, and the bend-not-break nature of the woody grass enables them to withstand pressures concrete and wood cannot.

In your plight to live a productive and healthy life, you must also endure the battle scars of trials and tribulations. Your strength—and resistance to strains and pressures—determines how long you can play the game, and how healthy you remain while playing it. Are you debilitated or inspired by challenges?

In the context of performance, strength relates to the ability to take action or get others to do it for you. People and companies rarely profit from ideas alone, they profit from *implemented*. And, like a credible entrepreneur or trial attorney, the strength of their ideas and theories are persuasive.

Finally, strength refers to your ability to resist work-related stress. You battle the physical stresses of travel and long workweeks, and the mental stress of managing multiple priorities, beating deadlines and tolerating business disappointments. Hans Selye, the Austrian endocrinologist, believed "What we call aging is nothing more than the sum total of all the scars left by the stress of life." If you are weak, a breeze extinguishes your flame; if you are strong, that same breeze fans your flames of ambition.

Versatility

Bamboo can be eaten, worn and used in landscape design
Bamboo's secretion, called tabashir,
is used to fight coughs and asthma
Bamboo is used to make ladders, clothes, boats,
furniture, flooring and paper

Sustainable success is possible if you remain versatile enough to modify your skills and tactics to different opportunities, audiences and technology. For instance, great communicators have the gift of versatile communication. Ronald Reagan could speak to world leaders, a television camera, his opponent in a debate, and the blue-collar worker at the mouth of a coalmine. He was effective in a suit, a tuxedo, or a ten-gallon cowboy hat while sitting on the front porch of his ranch. Any effective communicator must be able to tailor their message to different demographics, audience size and available time.

While most companies focus on a single brand message, they must remain versatile and resilient enough to adapt to changing customer demands, economic factors, and competitive strategies. Versatility implies the ability to move freely in all directions, or have competencies in many areas. One of the competencies high achievers share is the ability to utilize their talents when opportunities change form, flexible enough to rise to the occasion and not only tread water, but swim to safety.

Psychologist Al Siebert states, "Organizations need people who are resilient, people who can adapt quickly, change directions, and bounce back." Paul Stoltz, author of *Adversity Quotient,* suggests a person's success is tied to his ability to cope with adversity. Those people with "a high adversity quotient make more money, are more innovative and better problem-solvers than those less adept and handling misfortune," Like bamboo, those who bend and don't break, persevere.

Similarly, while people are often paid for a principal talent, they must also share a host of related talents such as communication, leadership, and creativity. Versatility equals mobility and compatibility with many opportunities. Versatility means you have more than one arena to demonstrate your talents. Sales people often share transferable talents (if you sell real estate, you can likely sell insurance, cars, or financial products.) Ron Howard demonstrates versatility in the entertainment industry as an actor, producer and director. Ongoing professional development enables versatility, survival and growth.

Companies seek diversity in their employee base because it enables versatility. When employees offer a variety of cultures, experiences, and languages, the company has a broader talent base they can offer their customers and business partners.

Contribution

*An acre of bamboo releases 35% more
oxygen than an acre of trees
Bamboo reverses the effects of global warming
It is an asset to its environment, not a liability*

When you contribute, you make your world a better place, and you appreciate the power of your accomplishments, creating a space in your life to receive more.

Medical missionary Dr. Albert Schweitzer said, "The only ones among you who will be really happy are those who will have sought and found how to serve." He is the 1952 Nobel Peace Prize winner who lived his philosophy of "doing something for somebody every day for which you do not get paid." His philosophy remains a respected thread in the fabric of our culture today. Your opportunity to contribute can be discovered or consciously identified.

In the right environment, bamboo grows quickly, and is constantly reaching for new, fertile ground with its "running" root system. It is gradually becoming a favored material in building and clothing materials. In 2008, car manufacturer Mitsubishi announced itself the first automaker to develop a technique using bamboo fibers in its cars' interiors for reinforcement. The use of petroleum plastics for the same purpose requires more energy to manufacture, creates significantly more waste and, later, costly recovery (reclamation) efforts. We have to thank Mitsubishi Motors for their creative contribution using bamboo's flexible fibers for the sake of safety, fuel- efficiency and clean air.

Using bamboo as manufacturing material promises to reduce CO_2 emissions by 28%. It is strong, light and environmentally responsible. Bamboo gives more than it takes, and the environment is healthier for hosting bamboo. Like the Boy Scout's mantra, "leave the campground better than you found it," companies and individuals now believe it *de rigueur* to "do their part" individually and collectively to make circumstances better than they found them.

Contribution is the attitude of gratitude. This inspiration to contribute stems from the recognition that your success is the product of your deliberate efforts that were expedited or guided by others who provided input, held open doors, and mentored. You didn't make it alone. You now have opportunities to match your "gifts" with similar gestures, giving back to the collective body of those striving for similar opportunities. The emotions created by *giving* have positive emotions and health ramifications.

A 2006 Johns Hopkins University study reveals that volunteering reduces stress and builds self-esteem. Alan Luks, author of *The Healing Power of Doing Good,* provides medical statistics illustrating how volunteering improves insomnia and strengthens the immune system. A1992 study of more than 3,000 volunteers, found that people who helped others regularly—meaning weekly—enjoyed less stress and experienced a greater sense of self-worth compared with those who volunteered only once a year. When professionals help clients and coworkers in a different or extra way, stress is reduced. Achievement is facilitated and more fulfilling when your efforts buoy the success and well-being of the lives of those around you.

Consider the *versatility* of *contribution.* You can give your time, talents, money, possessions, council or leadership to good causes. Opportunities are not limited to cash donations; small collective and collaborative efforts result in measurable changes. Great companies contribute to the wellness of the environment by "adopting a highway", reducing pollutants, and limiting intrusion on the environment wherever they build. Additionally, companies recycle wasted product materials, purchase recycled paper products, and encourage employees to recycle trash and bottles--even contribute unwanted toys to the less fortunate. They ensure their environment and community are better than how they found them.

Fortune Magazine ranked NetApp the best company to work for. NetApp gives employees five paid days of volunteer work. Genentech, the biotech leader, offers workers childcare and a fitness center. As of 2009, revenues are up 25%. The mutual balance of helping others yields measurable results. These programs improve employee retention, improved company morale, and team cohesiveness.

Contribution takes place anytime individuals work toward a common endeavor or objective. A great company is merely an assembly of great *people* who form teams, work together, and make contributions that lead to achievement. These contributions result in productivity, profits and industry presence. As a result, employees are more loyal and continue to make even greater contributions to their company.

You can live and give the three bamboo virtues, but you must first jettison past psychological baggage about the true extent of your potential by debunking myths and assumptions about personal growth and development.

Chapter 3

Three Myths about Potential

Potential is esoteric and obscure. Potential isn't "here," it's either within or in the beyond. Potential is like the future: it is always on the horizon. Potential is about what *could be* if you do the right things, and each day presents you with the opportunity to take steps or strides along your potential path.

Potential transcends gender, class, religion and ethnicity. We refer to our potential like we refer to a pile of money, yet it isn't concrete and physical, it is fluid and psychological. Potential refers to degrees of future growth, predicated on the presence of personal strengths. James W. Newman, author of *Release Your Brakes!,* says potential is "the present combination of one's system of talent, information, an inner motivation." Potential isn't a snapshot of a specific outcome, it's a kaleidoscope of possibilities.

When you tell someone, "You have tremendous potential," their mind often races to, "What's missing? What do you mean I have potential (for greatness), I'm not great now?" Some are delighted to learn they have plenty of stored potential, but curious about the span of road between them and "realized" potential. "Potential" implies work ahead, obstacles to be hurdled, and venturing into the unknown—a daunting endeavor for many. People frequently find it more convenient to appreciate "what is" instead of "what could be."

Potential remains ambiguous, elusive, and yet the quest of each success-oriented individual and results-oriented organization in America. We will discuss your most promising areas of potential—your talents—developing the skills for their release, and the motivation to make this endeavor a lifestyle and not an event.

The reason many people don't systematically embark on a quest to deliberately pursue personal change is due to a subconscious belief system that governs their behaviors and decisions. Based on a few myths and assumptions about talent, achievement, and the latitude of their options, people remain confined by past experiences, limited by self-imposed glass ceilings, and held hostage by shared notions of human potential.

Knowing the truths behind the myths allow you to recognize

- You don't need to wrestle with the status quo in life or a career
- Your future is bigger than your past
- Your talents can be cultivated and productively applied

You will be released from the golden handcuffs that bind you to satisfaction and complacency, and freed to pursue greater ambitions that thrill and fulfill.

Myth #1
Potential can be reached

Reality
Potential is a process, not a place

Tapping your potential is a journey, not a destination where you hang your hat and kick up your feet. Potential is a process of progressively realizing and utilizing your talents, but not necessarily in a single discipline. Your potential is transferable to a variety of contexts, and will yield results for those who pursue it.

If you feel "tapped out" in a job, it may have more to do with burnout, a bad manager, or a change in passion for your chosen career. Employment parameters do not limit your personal potential. When you feel you've outgrown your environment, move on. Find other places to establish your roots. M. Scott Peck, author of *The Road Less Traveled,* teaches, "Life is not a problem to be solved, but a mystery to be lived." Never fear change, embrace the adventure.

Michael Jordan may have reached his potential as a basketball star. He garnered 5 MVP awards, 14 NBA all-star appearances, and was later inducted into the Basketball Hall of Fame in 2009. However, after his three-peat of championships with the Chicago Bulls in 1991, 1992, and 1993, he was ready for his next adventure in baseball.

If you measure potential by degrees, Jordan had less to prove and perhaps only few degrees of room to grow in basketball, but plenty of potential in baseball—he didn't demonstrate the same prowess and skill in the game. (He batted a .202 with the Birmingham Barons, a Chicago White Sox farm team.) He later returned to the Bulls and led them to another three-peat in 1996, 1997 and 1998.

His potential in basketball had been revealed to a greater degree than his potential in baseball. He had plenty of room to grow in baseball had he stayed the course. The difference was simple: he put more hours of practice on the court than he had on the diamond. Though people often feel there is no room to grow within a single discipline, they may overlook the fact that personal potential extends to infinite opportunities in many varied arenas.

Bamboo doesn't die when harvested, and neither do you. Bamboo continuously grows new roots, shoots and culms, spreading to favorable environments—it's a dynamic gathering of continuous growth. While you can reach your potential within a job (there is nothing new or challenging left for you to do), your personal potential is forever blossoming and knows no boundaries.

Developing your potential is like pursuing your shadow: you advance, you do not conquer. Yet, it isn't a Sisyphean endeavor. Realizing your potential is a life-sustaining quest that sharpens skills, strengthens purpose and yields results.

My real estate agent learned to play the piano at age forty, got a Series 7 brokerage license at fifty, and a real estate license at age sixty. Virginia Adair, an award-winning poet, lived a full and accomplished life, finishing her last collection of poetry at age eighty-seven—and she was blind. These are examples of Bamboo People: always growing and persevering while living the virtues of Strength, Versatility and Contribution.

Potential is revealed through a series of achievements that should be celebrated frequently, not sandbagged for some future glorious day of recognition. Shakespeare said, "What's won is done / joys soul lies in the doing." Enjoy the pursuit of your academic, financial, professional, physical, and intellectual potential. Growth opportunities are everywhere. You can run out of years. You do not run out of potential.

Myth #2
Potential is unique to the talented

Reality
We are all talented and potential is universal

Potential implies stored power—in your case, power and ability for something productive. A bamboo shoot also has a lot of promise--it packs enormous potential if placed it in the right environment. When allowed to grow, it offers a myriad of practical applications. When individual talents are placed in the right environments (opportunities), the potential for making a myriad of productive contributions is universal. Like the song by America, "Oz never did give nothing to the Tin Man, that he didn't, didn't already have." You already possess talents and potential, you only need a process to develop the roots that enable that positive potential to flourish.

Potential is universal, but finding the best outlet for potential takes a strategy. High achievers proactively place their roots where they can thrive. They create more opportunities than they randomly encounter. Most people are talent rich, but opportunity poor. These opportunities must be identified, created and cultivated.

Michael Gotovac is a Croatian immigrant who came to the United States in 1964. Michael wasn't put on this earth to fix cars, sell computers or litigate. Michael is a talented people-person who enjoys working "front and center" as the bartender at Dan Tana's restaurant in West Hollywood, CA. He is a legend in town because he's been pouring drinks, telling jokes and feeding customers for 45 years.

Michael's talent base includes

1. Anticipating peoples' needs
2. Remarkable recall for names, food and beverage preferences
3. Multitasking and working efficiently—in several languages

When you sit at his bar and order their famous Beckerman Potatoes, ketchup appears before you can ask for it. Customers marvel at his ability to remember their "usual" cocktail, although they haven't been to the restaurant in five years. He does this with flair, a thick Croatian accent, and a charming, self-deprecating demeanor. His bar is full from opening until closing, with rows of people patiently waiting for an open barstool.

There are many who share his talents. Michael found unique ways to choreograph his talents and put them to productive use. His talents synergized, creating a talent-pattern that lent itself to his line of work; practice and experience enabled him to hone his talents to an art form. He has put his three boys though college and graduate school, and put smiles on the faces of loyal regulars, tourists and celebrities for decades. He continues to manifest and monetize his potential through the virtues of strength, versatility and contribution.

Myth #3
Potential develops vertically, along a ladder

Reality
Potential develops randomly, across a chessboard

You can grasp the next rung on the corporate ladder, and promote from director, to vice president and enjoy the increase in salary and benefits. This is a logical progression within a silo or stovepipe culture. However, potential isn't limited to ascending a prescribed hierarchy. What if you are self-employed? What if you have two jobs? What if you don't have a defined career track or appear to have finished the one you're on? Don't look up, look around.

Do You Run or Clump?

There are two general species of bamboo: running and clumping. Clumping bamboo makes new plants (culms) only a few inches from one another and remains a cohesive batch. Running bamboo spreads with new culms and shoots surfacing across a broader territory. How they grow is simply in the nature of the species itself. Similarly, people seem to fall in one of the two categories of runners or clumpers.

You may be a career clumper: a lawyer who stays with the same firm, demonstrates talent, and eventually arrives at the corner office as a partner. Clumpers can broaden their experience base, develop talents and reveal their potential while working for a single organization or discipline their entire lives.

Runners have a variety of talents they fearlessly explore, or they may have the attention span of a moth. They pursue new opportunities and careers swiftly, with little attachment to previous quests. Neither runner nor clumper is better than the other; it is merely a matter of dominant characteristics. It's like the analogy of the turtle and the racehorse: one isn't better than the other, but if you corral a racehorse, or push a turtle on the racetrack, neither will be happy.

Running bamboo can produce 200 poles because its rhizome roots are broad, not only deep. As the roots spread, they develop more shoots with their own root systems. They venture out, seeking new, fertile ground. Like your potential, they are *intensive* and *extensive*. They grow wherever given the opportunity. Similarly, your life may not advance along a track, it may maneuver along a grid, seeking multiple and varied opportunities.

Potential *can* be developed along a ladder, but think of your life and career as furnished with many ladders from which to choose, and they lean against many different structures. You aren't limited to climbing one ladder at a time—and you don't need to complete a ladder in order to move to the next. You are capable of lateral moves, diagonal moves, multiple or single-rung ascension, and even concurrent ascension along several ladders (think of training for a marathon while writing a book). You can take direct strides or a series of non-linear moves. These non-linear patterns make discovering potential more analogous to a maneuvering across a chessboard.

Profiles in Chess and Running Bamboo

Like the pawn, you sometimes take small steps, one square at a time. There are productive days when you move like a castle, making longer strides laterally, forward, or backward; like a knight, you creatively negotiate out of difficult situations, moving forward two squares and over another. Even a backward move is an offensive and productive move if you avoid trouble--what feels like *regression* in your life and career may be a temporary necessity to stop, focus, and turn *regression* into *progression.*

Ben Stein epitomizes a chessboard career. He is an author, humorist, economist, and actor, to list a few of his credentials. Ben Stein's interests run in many different directions, and he has the resume to prove it.

- Graduated from Columbia University with a degree in Economics in 1966
- Graduated from Yale Law School in 1970
- Speech writer for both Richard Nixon and Gerald Ford
- Columnist for the Wall Street Journal
- Commentator for CBS Sunday Morning
- He has published 51 books (business, satire)
- His game show, *Win Ben Stein's Money,* won 7 Emmy Awards
- Acted in movies, television and commercials (His role as the dull teacher in *Ferris Bueller's Day Off* ranks as one of the fifty most famous scenes in American Film)

His quirky demeanor and brainy sarcasm is entertaining. His varied interests and accomplishments exemplify the chessboard theory and "running" bamboo: significant accomplishments in unrelated professions and projects that span a forty-year career.

Wine First, Then We Golf

Ely Callaway is a "runner" born in LaGrange, Georgia and graduated from Emory University in 1940. He worked for Trust Company of Georgia and, at twenty-one, joined the Army as a reserve officer in the Quartermaster Corps.

After five years of military service, Callaway enjoyed a successful career in the textile industry, and in 1968 became president and director of Burlington Industries, Inc., the world's largest textile company. With his newfound capital, he pursued his next passion.

After establishing the Callaway Vineyard and Winery in Southern California in 1969, he sold the business in 1982 and bought Hickory Stick USA Inc., a small firm that manufactured and sold putters and specialty wedges. He built the brand into Callaway Golf, which patented unique products such as the "Big Bertha" driver and famous oversized irons. In a decade, the business grew from 5 million to 800 million dollars in sales, and, by 1996, it was the world's largest golf equipment company.

A Painting Paints a Thousand Words
Leonardo da Vinci created more than the Mona Lisa. He was an Italian polymath whose revolutionary concepts and inventions demonstrated the skills of diversely talented man. He didn't achieve great heights in a single discipline; he achieved legendary status in many disciplines. He was a "runner" who established his roots deep and wide in a variety of disciplines.

He was a

- Mathematician
- Engineer
- Inventor
- Anatomist
- Painter
- Sculptor
- Architect
- Botanist
- Musician
- Writer

He created the first robot, concept helicopter, and helped design St. Peter's Basilica. He was both physically and intellectually ambidextrous. He performed tasks simultaneously, could write backwards, read his notes in a mirror, and wrote music while inventing musical instruments. His math, art and science talents resulted in a magnificent legacy.

Jack and the Bamboo Cane

Jack Welch is a classic clumper. He is a bright guy from Peabody, Massachusetts who eventually earned a Ph.D. in Chemical engineering from The University of Illinois at Urbana-Champagne, and then joined GE in 1960. He almost left the company due to its legendary bureaucracy, but was convinced to stay by another executive who recognized Welch's significant potential.

He was a clumper and a climber. He enjoyed a series of promotions and eventually became Vice President in 1972, Senior Vice President in 1977, and Vice Chairman in 1979. He finally became GE's youngest CEO in 1981 and rose to stardom in the world of CEO performance. He was voted "Manager of the Century" by Fortune Magazine, and continues to teach for MIT and serve as a consultant to several Fortune 100 companies. Welch was quoted as saying, "My main job was developing talent. I was a gardener providing water and other nourishment to our top 750 people. Of course, I had to pull out some weeds, too."

Welch systematically built a future, and established his roots deep and wide within the structure of a billion-dollar organization. After a formal education (certainly an important part of foundation), he developed his talents, and worked tirelessly achieving his dream of becoming CEO. Welch is a bamboo executive.

Though many admire Welch's rise from middle class to stardom and wealth, few make it. They are enticed by the rewards and the wine, but are unwilling to stomp the grapes. Yet, there are no shortcuts. In today's world of immediate gratification, we have overlooked the truism that the only place you find success before work is in the dictionary. Your journey will be a labor of love if your talents and values fuel your plans.

The following chapters detail the seven roots that create the necessary foundation "running" or "clumping" success. You probably have already addressed these roots, perhaps merely out of order, or you've begun a similar process but lost momentum, focus, or passion.

The roots are sequenced for a reason: They help you avoid a ready, fire, aim approach to development and ensure momentum, enable you to remain focused, and sustain your passion as you experience daily progress.

Chapter 4

The Talent Root

Bamboo continually contributes its gifts

If a man has a talent and cannot use it, he has failed.
If he has talent and uses only half of it, he has partly failed.
If he has a talent and learns somehow to use the whole of it,
He has gloriously succeeded, and won a satisfaction and a
triumph few men ever know.

--Thomas Wolfe

"Talent" originally referred to a monetary measurement. Babylonians' and Sumerians' monetary system used shekels, minas and talents as currency. In today's market, a talent would be worth about a thousand dollars. Money is intrinsically useless until exchanged for something of value. If your talents lie dormant and are not put to productive use, you only possess *stored power*. It's like the line from the movie *A Bronx Tale*: "The saddest thing in life is wasted talent."

The Biblical story of talents is told as The Parable of the Talents (Matthew 25: 14-30): A man goes on a journey and trusts his three servants with his talents. He gave the first servant five talents, the second received two talents, and the third received one talent. Each used their talents differently.

The man who had five talents put them to work and yielded five more talents; the man with two talents put them to work and gained two more; the man who received a single talent, dug a hole and hid it until his master returned.

When the master returned, he was pleased with the servants who put the talents to good use. He was furious with the servant who did nothing with it. His single talent was taken away and given to the servant who now had ten talents. The lesson was clear: "For everyone who has will be given more, and he will have abundance. Whoever does not have, even what he has will be taken from him."

The parable isn't about making money; it's about your moral responsibility to put your talents to productive use, and the likely regrets if you don't. As Galileo said, "I do not feel obliged to believe that the same God who has endowed us with sense, reason and intellect has intended us to forgo their use." It's not about a life of riches; it's about how applied talents enrich your life. Allowing your talents to lie dormant is like putting your sundial in the shade.

In the spirit of bamboo, make time each day to develop your talents although you may not see immediate results. Each day you apply yourself, you strengthen your root system, nearing certain growth. Your root system is constantly trying to secure itself for the new personal heights you will achieve.

3D Talent

Talents are the seedbed of your potential. If your talents are not cultivated, you will not live your true potential. If you put your talents to work, which is your calling, you discover more of your potential on a daily basis. You experience the greatest growth—and make the greatest contribution—if you

1. Discover your talents
2. Develop your talents
3. Deliver your talents

--in the context of productivity and contribution.

When people speak of talents, they use words like "special, natural, and unique." Yet, talents are not special or unique per se, because many people share your talents. If you are musically inclined, you can find others that share the same talents. What's unique is the degree to which your talents are developed and applied.

You know what you are good at and the activities you enjoy, and these are the most promising areas of cashing in on your potential because

- You are naturally drawn to the activities and many of these inborn abilities reveal themselves to you during childhood
- You enjoy the activities—which ensures you willingly invest time in their development
- You feel rewarded, enriched and fulfilled when you have time to pursue your talent-based activities

Your chances of succeeding increase when you develop a talent rather than invest time repairing obvious weaknesses. Yet, our culture is obsessed with mending flaws in how we look and perform. Look at the breadth of titles and sales of the popular *"For Dummies"* series and—more self-deprecating—*"The Complete Idiot's Guide to . . ."* These books address popular skills such as using PowerPoint, to niche subjects such as *PHP and MySQL Web Development All-In-One Desk Reference for Dummies.* We seem to acknowledge our talents, but are preoccupied by our weaknesses. I have been an avid consumer of professional development books for twenty years—and even written a few. There *is* value in balancing your portfolio of personal skills, and satisfying a curiosity for

- what makes communication clear
- what makes a negotiator effective
- what makes people productive

However, it is naïve to assume you will move the needle from poor performance to peak performance, and feed your family and your future on what was once a weakness. All the research points to your strengths as the most fertile ground to plant your seeds, establish your roots, and enjoy the riches brought forth.

Delegation--what companies do with their "business partners"--is the most efficient means for you to remain focused on your passion, while off-loading work that slows your momentum and kills your spirit. One man's poison is another man's food. Your dread of of balancing a ledger is embraced by a left-brainer who studied finance and accounting in college.

Peter Drucker, author of *The Effective Executive* said, "Effective people make strength productive." It's not about shunning responsibilities; it's about investing a larger percentage of time in

- Activities where you excel
- On the work you enjoy
- In environments where you thrive

If these talent patterns and opportunities don't immediately reveal themselves to you, a discussion with a coach/mentor/trusted advisor about your talents and goals will be very helpful and is addressed in the next chapter.

Build an Empire on a Single Talent

Frank Sinatra never wrote a lyric and could not play an instrument. He was a singer. From the moment he first opened his mouth in song as a child, and people dropped a few pennies in the jar on the piano where he sat, he knew he had the raw materials upon which to base a career. He was not distracted by attempts to balance his portfolio of skills taking piano, guitar, or clarinet lessons. He had other interests, but he proportionately invested the greatest amount of time in his greatest strength: his voice, his interpretation of lyrics and his delivery. Like most high achievers, he collaborated with those who demonstrated the talents he was missing: great musicians like Tommy Dorsey, Duke Ellington, and Louis Armstrong; and great songwriters like Cole Porter, Jimmy Van Heusen, and Stephen Sondheim. They each brought their separate talents to the table, and together formed a legendary synergy with unmatched legacies.

True, because Frank was Frank, he was an asset to many projects in entertainment and was a very quick study (watch him dance with Gene Kelly, or act in *From Here to Eternity*, for which he won an Academy Award.) However, few race to buy a stack of Frank Sinatra films. It is his voice and stage performance that perseveres.

Great companies and high achievers follow the same pattern. Companies outsource others to do the work for which they are not prepared, or because another company simply has unmatched expertise. If the resources aren't in-house, then *resourcefulness* can solve your problems. The great college basketball coach John Wooden tells us "don't let what you cannot do interfere with what you can do."

High achievers collaborate with those who have ready-made talents to deliver. When technology skills hinder your great ambitions, hire someone who can help. Most professional speakers I know admit they can't build a PowerPoint presentation. They focus on content and delivery, not the technical aspects of rendering clever slides. The speaker quickly sketches their slides on sheets of paper with a Sharpie, gives them to the PowerPoint genius, which are later emailed back to the speaker. The hours of training and practice required to be fluent in PowerPoint is better invested in other aspects of communication. I believe in learning and growing at every opportunity, but time invested in filling your talent gaps is done at the expense of time invested in other ready-to-deliver skills. When your professional focus is on what you enjoy (personally gratifying), what you do well (a talent that produces results), and what you can monetize (there is a market for it), you can generate great levels of income and enjoyment.

You Can Monetize a Hobby

Karen is a colleague who makes a great living designing curriculum for her clients. She takes complex learning objectives, draws out the essence of the learning points, and arranges them in a teachable storyline. She expresses educational ideas in ways that are memorable and engaging for the students.

The origin of the word "curriculum" has its roots in the Latin word for "course of action, race, or chariot." She builds a learning path for students that tells a story and arrives at pre-determined outcomes. Well-designed curriculum makes the instructor's job easier, and the students learning experience more enjoyable. I asked Karen how she found this line of work and why she enjoys it:

"I was an English major in college with plans to teach after I graduated. I also read a lot of poetry. I was fascinated at how complex ideas and stories were pared-down to a couple of stanzas. We had assignments in class that required us to write a one-page essay about an experience (falling in love, growing older, the beauty of a sunrise). The second phase of the assignment was to reduce our elaborate essay to a fourteen-line sonnet—weed-out unnecessary words without losing the intent of the essay. I enjoyed the challenge of turning prose into poetry. Michelangelo said, 'I saw the angel in the marble and I carved until I set him free.' I compared the essay to a block of marble and I chiseled away anything that wasn't the sonnet. Today, the work is the same: take pages of instruction and elicit the essence of the learning, add designs or illustrations that clarify the idea, and sequence the pages."

Karen uses her honed talent for analysis, word play, and "story structure," in conjunction with her value for teaching, education and learning. She found that her talents are transferable, and the skills they form can be exploited in a variety of contexts and circumstances. She identified something she enjoyed, and found a career that enables her to express those values and talents.

Your talents are most productively identified through meaningful communication with someone about your career choices and projects. A dialogue-driven discussion surfaces the raw materials you need to succeed.

Bamboo Review

- Applied talents enrich your life
- It is better to pursue a talent/strength than to fix a weakness
- High achievers collaborate with others who fill their talent gaps

Chapter 5

The Communication Root

Bamboo knows where to establish its roots

Our chief want in life is somebody who will makes us do
what we can.
-Ralph Waldo Emerson

The Communication Root is the second root in the sequence
and doesn't only address the quality of your communication,
but emphasizes the importance of taking time to
communicate your qualities.

Discussing your talents with a coach/mentor/trusted advisor
is the most effective way to identify your talents, and
determine which one(s) should be pursued. You think you
know what makes you tick, but until you challenge yourself
to express those talents in detail, you are close-but-not-clear.
If you are not clear, you can only approximate the kind of
work that enables your roots to thrive.

Speaking with a coach/mentor/trusted advisor facilitates the
clarification process. If you work with a dedicated coach,
they are likely a database of research and resources that will
help you in your quest. Your coach provides a different
worldview and experience base you can't access if you work
alone. Moreover, when you share ideas, you create a sense
of urgency and accountability for their completion. This
should be a series of ongoing conversations conducted at
regular intervals to sustain your motivation and keep you on
track. If you merely identify great ideas and do not
implement, your conversations are futile.

Find someone willing to dedicate time and attention to this discussion, and you will illuminate your skills, talents and fertile ground for their growth. In the words of Socrates, you will "know thyself."

Here are the three steps to identifying your talents:

1. A Talent Talk
2. Avoid the Vague
3. Dynamic Listening

A Talent Talk

This is not a casual chat while running errands or having a beer. This is a scheduled, sit-down meeting, free from distractions, dedicated to discovering your passions. The key is *positioning*. It is unproductive to broach the talent talk on Friday afternoon in an elevator as your chosen coach clutches their car keys. Wrong time, wrong place, wrong mindset. You must state your purpose, and ask for a day and time.

"I'd like to get your help and feedback about my some of my professional development and goals for next year. When do you have an hour this week to meet for coffee?"

This helps them understand the purpose of your call, the nature of the subject matter and the time required to be productive. Psychologist Robert Sternberg calls this "practical intelligence: knowing what to say to whom, knowing when to say it, and knowing how to say it for maximum effect." This sets proper expectations, and allows you to choose a meeting place conducive to clear communication.

During this discussion, you will recognize talent combinations that synergize and form job or activity descriptions and new opportunities. Progress begins the moment you identify your talents and strengths, and begin actively seeking opportunities to put them to work. It is the equivalent of finding the perfect place to establish your bamboo colony.

The International Coach Foundation surveyed 210 coaching clients and identified the most popular purposes coaches serve: 84.8% use the role of a coach as a sounding board; 78.1% use a coach to solve motivational issues; 84.5% to solve time management issues; and 74.3% for career guidance. When you actively seek the advice of others, you dramatically increase your experience base by tapping into the combined intellectual capital of those involved. Additionally, when you have the opportunity to express your thoughts, you can more readily distinguish between the vital and the trivial, and think like a rifle, not a shotgun. That's the value of heeding others' perspectives.

Ongoing coaching discussions keep you focused, motivated, and aligned with the right activities. You have too many ideas circling your head to sort them only through thinking— it's like trying to herd cats. Your great ideas are further stimulated and organized through structured, supportive discussions, complete with pen and paper. Your coach enables you to separate the wheat from the chaff, and the confidence to get started on the isolated priorities that make a difference.

Avoid the Vague

During job interviews, candidates mistakenly discuss their talents and strengths in vague language. "I'm really good with people" makes me wonder, "Do you really have a choice?" Lee Iacocca said, "You'd' better get along with people, because that's all we have around here." You're good with what kind of people (students, the elderly, those with special needs)? Or, you're good with people in what context (teaching, consulting, building relationships)? Adjectives like "self-starter, out-of-the-box thinker, organized and assertive" cast broad nets, and fail to capture specifics. Most job candidates express platitudes in stained-glass attitudes. The purpose of your coaching discussion is to get beyond trite generalities.

Your talents should not be merely discussed and acknowledged: explore them, take them apart, hold them up to the light. Shake it like a wrapped birthday gift, trying to identify the contents. "I love dogs" doesn't have the "handles" you need to embrace new opportunities. Should you breed dogs, volunteer to place abandoned dogs in good homes, or own a dog walking business? If you say you want to do something in technology, it's like saying you want to do something that involves electricity. Drill further until the parts assemble a clear picture.

Think about how many different careers require the following skills and talents:

- Analytical skills
- Creative skills
- Listening skills

A good CPA has all three; so does an advertising executive. How do these lend themselves to the kind of work that would make you leap out of bed on Mondays? Would you like to sell sports cars? Would you prefer to sell luxury homes? Match your talents with your passions and you have a formidable recipe for success. You're trying to move the needle from

- Being busy to being effective
- From satisfied to gratified
- From maintenance mode to growth mode

Choose a person and a place to have a productive conversation for this potentially defining moment.

The Devil You Know

Ask your coach to play devil's advocate. (A professional career coach should know this). Ask them to question you and drill beneath the flat surface of platitudes. You will grasp the essence and context of your greatest gifts when pushed to respond to clarifiers such as

- Where?
- How?
- In what way?
- How often?
- With whom?

Unless your coach drills further, your personal assessments will be just-left-of center, just a tad out of tune. When you say "creative," your coach should ask how, where, and under what circumstances. Do you solve problems creatively, write poetry, or can you draw a caricature of your boss? Continue the exercise until you have identified the talents that surface most frequently, most naturally, and feel the most rewarding.

Similarly, if your coach speaks in generalities, draw them down to specifics. Don't be afraid to push them to places of clearer expression. If they say, "I noticed you like to design things," ask, "what things?" If you are complimented for your analytical skills, ask for specific examples. Put your coach on the hot seat, and enjoy an even exchange of ideas that uncover solutions. This is the epitome of two people engaged in a meaningful conversation on a single theme, not merely a monologue in the presence of another person. It is both discovery and affirmation.

Develop deeper dialogue with drill-downs like

- How do you mean?
- Describe that for me . . .
- In what context?
- Tell me more . . .
- What sorts of activities?
- What makes it difficult for you?
- How are you handling that now?
- What thoughts do you have about . . .

This is the time to be interested, not interesting. Instead of asking closed-ended questions that elicit simple, brief answers, like

"Do you get along well with your boss?" Ask, "Tell me about your relationship with your boss."

Instead of "Isn't that difficult to do?" You can ask, "How would I go about getting that done?"

"Is that a reasonable goal for me?" is better phrased, "What do you think about me pursing that goal?"

If they say, "I don't think you would enjoy the process," avoid making a quick assumption such as "is it the long hours or the people I work with? If you want an unbiased answer without leading them, simply ask, "Why is that?"

The intention of your ongoing communication is to draw out as much valuable information and brainstorming as possible. At the end of your discussion, be sure to ask,
"What do you think are my next steps?" or "If you were in my shoes, what would you do next?"

Coaching discussions should conclude with identified action items, dates for their completion, and a follow-up date to discuss progress.

Dynamic Listening

Dynamic listening is the process of getting physically into character in order to absorb, understand and empathize with every delivered word. Don't fold your hands on the table and nod your head at each worthy idea; scribble notes diligently on a pad of paper, capturing every idea. Your time will be more productive if you fully immerse yourself in the conversation. Writing requires you to more clearly express your thoughts and paint a picture of your talent base. Writing breeds more writing. When your ideas are in writing, it is easier to prioritize, eliminate or elaborate. You can structure your thoughts with bullets, highlighters and underscores. Your notes can now be merged, synthesized, distilled—and later reviewed.

It is nearly a waste of time to simply hear your coach's suggestions. "Hearing" only means that you are capable of perceiving sound in your immediate environment. You not only hear the words spoken by your coach, you also hear background music, car alarms, ringing phones, a distant television, and a host of ambient noise. The jewels of ideas you discover together must be documented. Unless you turn your concentration to the art of *listening*, you will miss many of your coach's words and their intended meaning. Dynamic listening builds the bridge to greater comprehension and retention.

A Talent Talk illuminates your path to well-matched projects and goals, and prevents you from adopting goals that sound good, fun, sexy, but are a poor match for your genuine zeal, values, and talents. It enables you to discover who you want to be and what you must do.

Bamboo Review

- A coach/mentor/trusted advisor will enable you to "know thyself"
- Coaching and communication is valuable when you drill to specifics
- Listening is a physical and mental exercise, facilitated by taking notes

Chapter 6

The Value Root

Bamboo makes positive contributions to its environment

"Things which matter most must never be at the mercy of things which matter least."

Goethe

Greg is a facilitator and business consultant living outside of Chicago. As he sits in a small, regional airport drinking bottled water, he catches up on the day's newspaper. It is now nine p.m., and his flight has been delayed an hour due to weather challenges. He is scheduled to land at O'Hare around eleven p.m., where he will take a shuttle bus to his car parked off airport property, and then drive thirty miles home. His head will likely hit his pillow by one a.m. Greg makes good money, he enjoys the nature of his work, but Greg is not happy.

Greg is my former colleague whose name was changed for this story. He has been married for ten years and has two children. His business is robust and the source of many financial freedoms, yet also the source of his angst. He has missed a few significant social occasions with his wife, and a few of his daughter's piano recitals. As he sits in the nearly deserted airport, he thoughtfully weighs the value of his chosen career against the sacrifices it demands.

Abraham Maslow said, "A musician must make music, an artist must paint, a poet must write, if he is to be ultimately at peace with himself." While Greg's work has intrinsic value, it has forced some of his personal values further down his list. His choices and sacrifices have created a diminishing return on investment. When he evaluated what mattered most to him, he found his career demands minimized the time he preferred to dedicate to his top priorities such as family and fitness. Subsequently, he explored new ways to pursue his passions, and found similar work that enabled his true priorities to receive top billing.

Greg demonstrated the versatility of bamboo when he found a new way to enjoy the same work. He now manages the training and development division for a great company fifteen miles from his home. He is able to teach, coach, and participate in the professional development needs of a thousand employees through workshops and webinars. He has lost his "status" at his favorite hotel chain and his preferred airline, but now enjoys prime time with his family at dinner and weekends. The financial rewards, pound for pound, are not as great, but his life is far more rewarding and he is happy.

Many people empathize with Greg's decisions, but Greg did something about it. Well done is better than well said. The change enables him to dedicate his energies to building a life and career without conflicting schedules and emotions. When there is conflict, you suppress your talents, your emotions are mixed, and your aggregate "life satisfaction index" is diminished by poor relationships, guilt an inner conflict. His talent seeds are now planted in a territory close to home where they can thrive, sustained by personal gratification, unencumbered by guilt and reluctance.

Values Defined

Values are a set of beliefs for which you demonstrate passion and view as meaningful. Values run the gamut from simple importance, such as a value for making good on promises and punctuality, to giving to the less fortunate and volunteering time for worthy causes. Many organizations now share corporate values for saving the planet through "green initiatives" and create products made from recycled materials, in biodegradable packaging with materials that lower manufacturing emissions. When your talents are fueled by the passion of clearly identified values, you have a formidable recipe for success. If you participate in causes, companies or a culture that conflict with your value system, you will never discover your true potential. When you promote a product, movement or personal mission that is truly satisfying, you add extra cylinders and a few hundred horsepower to your ambition and enthusiasm. In the bamboo world, this is nourishment for you root system.

Work should be a manifestation of your talents, an expression of your personal interests, and a source of satisfaction. Volunteer for roles at work that inspire you and choose careers that align with your personal standards. When you are not clear about your top priorities, you risk oscillating between career goals and personal choices without making measurable strides in either category. You will noodle around with the idea of getting your MBA with the same superficial interest as you fumble with your banjo. Don't swing blindfolded at a piñata; base your activities and goals on carefully considered choices that stir your emotions and strengthen you.

Roy Posner, author of *The Miraculous Phenomenon of Life Response*, suggests, "Implementing values energizes everything concerned with it. For an individual, committing to and applying values releases fresh energies, which always attract success, achievement, and well-being." When you perform tasks from a source of passion—and not simple duty—you have boundless energy and work becomes recreation.

There are a multitude of activities you enjoy and precious little discretionary time to pursue them. Prioritization eliminates the fluff, and focuses your attention on the right activities. Prioritizing your values doesn't address absolute importance, it evaluates temporary, *relative* importance. Your choices do not always eliminate, they re-sequence, and ensure your remain on your potential path.

Your values are not a static list of predictable priorities; they are a dynamic list readily affected by life events, experience and growth. Miller and deBaca's book *Quantum Change, When Epiphanies and Sudden Insights Transform Ordinary Lives*, calls this
"Seeing the light." Life events, big and small, can trigger a reorganization of your values which may affect the kind of work you do, where you do it, and how often.

Ongoing consideration about your talents and values are essential. This is not a frozen compass; it is an active radar screen influenced by relationships, age, financial circumstances, and a host of unforeseen life changes.

Transportation and Values

A friend of mine is a motorcycle enthusiast, but when he got married—and planned to have children—he had to rethink his values. He admitted that, as a bachelor, if he cracked his melon, it was his to crack, and few people were dependent on his ability to go to work and return with a paycheck. Now his melon is "community property," and people will depend on it to provide, feed, supply, and house them. He sold his motorcycles and now places his value for adventure in safer, more predictable arenas.

Merging Values and Restraints

In the 1950's the CEO of Volvo had a passion for safety. He lost a relative in a car accident and resolved to make vehicles safer. His primary motivation was innovation in the context of life-saving technology. He recruited Nils Ivar Bohlin, an engineer who developed ejection seats for SAAB fighter aircraft in the 1950's. Bohlin's task was formidable. After working with four-point harnesses found in fighter jets, he understood their value and their limitations for automobiles. However, together they engineered a simple solution still used in cars today: the three-point safety restraint. Volvo introduced it in 1959, and it soon became the standard with all brands. Millions of lives have been saved since its inception. The three-point safety restraint is a classic example of what happens when people with similar values and complimentary talents join to change the world.

Talent without Values

Michael Milken was enormously talented. He was a bright student from the San Fernando Valley in Los Angeles, who attended the Hass School of Business of the University of California, Berkley and later received his Master's degree in Business Administration from the University of Pennsylvania's Wharton School of Business.

Milken developed and expanded the use of high yield debt (junk bonds) in mergers and acquisitions, which fueled the 1980s boom in leveraged buyouts and hostile takeovers. Milken had a talent for financial innovation, though it was misguided. He enjoyed making money--not for others as most financial advisors would, but for himself (paying himself 500 million dollar year-end bonuses.) The companies he "partnered" with defaulted on their debt, or were bankrupt by 1990. Each savings and loan that purchased large shares of Milken's junk bonds was declared insolvent. He left a legacy of ruined companies and people.

Michael Milken was a bright individual who misapplied his talents. His values and ethics were also upside-down. Careers built on crooked motives, sinister business plans and heartless tactics are short-lived with long-term consequences.

The roots he planted in the subjects he studied so diligently were soon thwarted. Ironically, in keeping with the chess board theory, his potential wasn't forever frozen on a ladder. After serving 22 months in prison, he maneuvered in the new direction of philanthropy in education and medicine.

Big Hack Attack

Kevin Mitnick was a talented computer hacker and self-proclaimed "hacker poster boy." His crimes were highly publicized and the Department of Justice had him on their most wanted list. His criminal feats were detailed in the movies *Freedom Downtime* and *Takedown.*

Before Mitnick perfected his craft, he began by determining how to get free transportation by manipulating the Los Angeles bus punch card system. He eventually performed grander tasks, earning him a conviction for breaking into Digital Equipment Corporation's network and pilfering software. He hacked his way into about 35 major international corporations, costing millions in lost productivity.

After serving five years in prison, he was released in 2000, and, like any good Hollywood movie, the government again pursued him—this time offering him a career as a consultant to prevent similar crimes. (I guess it does take a thief to catch a thief.) His talents are real, the application was false. Talents, whether unused or misused, can be resurrected or corrected. He "repotted" his roots in lucrative soil. Today, he's a computer security consultant, author and speaker.

Balancing Values

Effective managers recognize that their team doesn't have a personal and a professional life; teams members have one life with personal and professional duties. If a team member is battling personal challenges, they will not fully engage in their work. Reach out when possible. When employees cannot make time for important matters—high priorities—they feel *imbalanced*. This inner-conflict distracts from high productivity and can only be resolved through blocking out time to address the issue.

Ask what you can do to help fellow employees perform at optimal levels, and ensure they can manage around personal issues that become "performance baggage." They will appreciate your management versatility and understanding during trying times; additionally, they will be more productive, and you will forge a lasting allegiance in your professional relationship.

Some companies offer day care facilities, cash machines, dry cleaners and other conveniences that lift the burden of managing a career and personal life. I worked with a company that invited a mobile car washing company to visit their offices every Friday. If employees want their car washed, they fill out a tag with their car description and license plate, attach it to their car keys, and put it in a shoebox. The valet finds their car in the parking lot, washes and vacuums the car, and returns the keys to a different shoebox. Driving a clean car is therapeutic and saves each employee almost an hour during their coveted weekend.

These minor conveniences free-up employees' calendars, enables them to enjoy their discretionary time and achieve balance in their routine.

Align Your Behavior

Align your talents with your chosen career and hobbies. A failure to align passion and profession is not due to running out of time or having too much on your plate. This isn't a time management obstacle. The alignment "disconnect" is due to a breakdown in *strategic thinking*. We work harder at the same things although they don't produce desired outcomes. Rather than work harder at your past activities, it may be time to pick new activities--which brings us to our next challenge.

Stabilize and strengthen your root system by choosing work and activities you enjoy. Find careers (or assignments) that inspire you. You may be exhilarated by risk, while others are debilitated by it. It is possible to work in the right industry, but fail to perform the right kind of work. (You are a manager who misses the "thrill of the kill" sales game). These are not difficult steps; they only require you to muster the motivation to take them. Communicate to your managers, coworkers and—if you have one—your coach. Take time to express your interest in new opportunities that enable you apply your talents more frequently. This is part of achievement's rich tapestry: the ongoing need to manage and develop yourself so you can utilize your greatest talents and take longer strides along your potential path. The more you succeed, the greater the resource you become to your organization and others. You will find yourself in a unique position to help others, buoy those in need of advice, and make greater contributions that lead to a significant personal legacy.

When you can't find an opportunity to use your natural talents, you feel like a square peg forever trying to fit into round-hole job descriptions. It reminds me of George Gobel's comment to Johnny Carson when Dean Martin and Bob Hope surprised the audience by crashing the show and joining them on the dais: "Did you ever feel life was a tuxedo and you were a pair of brown shoes?" Find a talent/career ensemble that makes sense.

Right Place, Right Time

I enjoy teaching. I enjoy the opportunity to find clear examples and demonstrations, and watch someone move the needle from inability to competency. It was as much fun to teach as to learn. It is rewarding.

When I stumbled upon the opportunity to work in the speaking and consulting business, I instantly saw this as a chance to get paid for talents I demonstrated naturally. Standing "front and center" for six hours a day felt natural and energizing. I learned later in my career through talent assessment instruments, that I am fascinated and intrigued by excellence—both watching people who demonstrate excellence at their craft (athletes, musicians, actors) and the process of achieving excellence in my own efforts. When you combine the operative words in my childhood talents (center-stage, speaking, teaching, performing, creativity, leading, self-expression, and laughter) with what I later discovered professionally (I'm challenged and intrigued by making good things great), a career that requires these talents, while helping others, was too good to be true. It was a vacation within a vocation. As I've noted in this chapter, value-driven talent applications are powerful, and we'll explore this further in the next chapter.

Bamboo Review

- Values should guide your decisions and will ensure sustainable success
- When values and activities are aligned, you stir your emotions and enjoy your work
- Personal values can evolve and reprioritize over time

Chapter 7

The Purpose Root

Bamboo grows with purpose everyday
Upward and outward
The extensive network of rhizome roots—
A highly active and complex root system--
Strengthens its foundation while ascending
To its full potential

Bamboo' purpose is to grow, expand, and survive. This purpose is life sustaining, and so powerful that bamboo grows in arid regions where draughts cause other crops to fail; and from low wetlands to high elevations in the mountains, bamboo soars to incredible heights while preserving moisture in the soil without the help of fertilizer, pesticides or herbicides. As Nietzsche states, "He who has a why to live can bear with almost any how."   Great companies and high achievers possess the same durable and hearty characteristics.

Nothing galvanizes your will and your determination more than a clear purpose. With purpose, your efforts are not performed in a vacuum; they are performed and appreciated in the broader context of their power and positive ramifications, driven by vision and passion, sustained by rewards and recognition. This is accurately represented by the story of The Three Bricklayers:

Three bricklayers are working together and a passerby by asks what they're doing. The first bricklayer replies, "I'm laying bricks, making $25 an hour." The second bricklayer replies, "I'm building a wall."   The third replies, "I'm building a Cathedral, and, one day, my daughter will be married here."

When your work is understood and respected in terms of its social significance--and even legacy--you access new reserves of energy, resolve, focus, determination and constancy of purpose. Purpose, coupled with action, has the power to change the world.

Programming Your Purpose

Viktor Frankl, author of *Man's Search for Meaning,* writes clearly about the importance of purpose, not only in terms of goal setting, but as a life-preserving mechanism. A theory he developed while imprisoned in a Nazi concentration camp, Logotherapy states that without a purpose, we die; when we no longer look forward to tomorrow, something inside us dies. Conversely, you feel very "alive" when each day has meaning; you have more energy, enthusiasm, and a better attitude.

His theory of living with purpose includes the following three tenets:

1. Creativity: the opportunity for the self-expression of our talents
2. Experiencing: interacting with the outside world through various relationships
3. Attitude: Choose your attitude, it is not determined by external circumstances

These tenets are a product of choice, not chance. A discussion about your talents and values should result in an inspiring endeavor—a project or goal that puts your talents in play while interacting with others. The byproduct is a natural optimism, enthusiasm and engagement.

Living and working with purpose eliminates distractions. Purpose prevents you from becoming a "success opportunist," shifting from one opportunity to the next without making any progress. You concentrate your energies on the particular, not the general. You are no longer a clock-watcher, but someone immersed in their work with the focus, "flow state," and the intention of a bricklayer building a cathedral.

Whether we call them our resolutions, goals, dreams, or tasks, it is essential to have an agenda every day that is a part of a bigger picture: A to-do list that is tied to your goals. The motivation to pursue these objectives is what keeps you healthy and alive. Purpose provides the motivation to want to tap your potential and is the answer to "what to do with what you have."

People often express goals without any passion or true intention to begin the work. It's as if we try to win approval or admiration by conceiving and sharing lofty goals. If the idea is pressed further with questions like "how" or "when," the discussion dies on the spot. "I'd like to start my own company" sounds great. But if you have nothing calendared, no business plan, no product or inventory, or even a target list of clients to work with, your "goal" is only an aspiration or distant notion. Without a basic plan of attack on paper, your expressed goal is an empty pipe dream. To firmly resolve each New Year to fix a problem, only until the emotion of making the decision fades, is a deliberate exercise in futility. If you're not passionate—even obsessed—by your sense of purpose, you will lose interest the day you experience your first challenge.

In *Psycho-Cybernetics*, Maxwell Maltz suggests that goals are not achieved and problems are not solved unless there is first a "burning desire" to do so. One of the greatest discoveries people make when trying change their lives is the importance of letting go of goals they never truly intended to accomplish, and ceasing to pursue activities they dislike.

Why join the health club only to find yourself regrettably getting dressed for the gym, dreading the drive, cursing the parking situation, counting the minutes—seconds—until you can leap of the treadmill and return home to the activities that you'd rather be doing. Are there other ways to stay fit?

If you think of ways to do the absolute minimum only so you can "check the box" and push the activity back under the carpet, you are not on your Potential Path. If you associate "goal setting" with "sacrifice, discipline, restraint, and pain," you are on a reluctant uphill battle. How would circumstances improve if you pursued goals that stirred positive emotions such as "love, fun, intrigue, excitement, entertaining, cool"—goals to which you are instinctively drawn?

Your potential path is paved with your talents and your interests, not the inherited goals of previous generations or the commercially sanctioned goals discussed on morning talk shows. The decision to accomplish a goal should begin with an inventory of activities you naturally enjoy and will eagerly pursue. They can be a labor of love, fraught with challenges, yet satisfying and rewarding. The goals you choose can be personal or professional, short- or long-range, artistic or scientific, but they must have one attribute in common: they must be *yours*. They must be a natural outgrowth of your personal enthusiasm, zeal, and talents. Think of activities to which you are intuitively drawn, have the energy for, and are gratified—even energized—when you are finished. These are the activities that intrigue and stimulate you enough that any obstacles that surface will be treated simply as entertaining puzzles that must be solved.

If you bounce these off your coach/mentor/trusted advisor, they will not only help you distinguish between fantasy and reality, they will facilitate a discussion around logical steps for their accomplishment and help you get the promotion, the new job, or participate in a business venture.

In his seminal work, *Flow: The Psychology of Optimal Experience,* Mihaly Csikszentmihalyi states that you are happiest when you are in a state of flow—a state of concentration and total immersion with your work. You don't seem to notice your surroundings, you're not easily distracted from your work. In an interview with Wired Magazine, Csíkszentmihályi describes flow as "being completely involved in an activity for its own sake. The ego falls away. Time flies. Every action, movement, and thought follows inevitably from the previous one, like playing jazz. Your whole being is involved, and you're using your skills to the utmost." Flow is a state where interest, immersion and enjoyment synergize and result in pure satisfaction. As Heraclitus so deftly states, "Man is most nearly himself when he achieves the seriousness of a child at play."

If you can experience these emotions while on your potential path, you will remain optimistically fixed on the road ahead—embracing its challenges, rewards and possibilities. And because you are centered on your passions, you enjoy the inherent peaks and plateaus of personal growth. This is the soil where your roots have the greatest potential and growth is guaranteed.

Talent-driven Purpose & Engagement

The Conference Board, a non-profit research organization, defines employee engagement as "a heightened emotional connection that an employee feels for his or her organization, that influences him or her to exert greater discretionary effort to his or her work." When you enjoy your work, and understand the "rules and how the game is played," it is far more engaging than working in a reactive environment without objectives, rewards or feedback.

The top three drivers for engagement include:

- Trust and integrity – how well managers communicate and "walk the talk"
- The nature of the job--is it mentally stimulating day-to-day?
- The connection between employee performance and company performance – does the employee understand how their work contributes to the company's overall performance?

Additionally, individual values play a part is what is viewed as engaging. For example, employees under age 44 rank "challenging environment/career growth opportunities" much higher than do older employees, who value "recognition and reward for their contributions." Your talents and value-driven goals should naturally engage you in their pursuit. You don't need reminders to stay on track, you are drawn there independent of external circumstances.

Team-Talent Goals

Managers have a more complex task. Managers must choreograph the talents of many people in different roles, and focus them on goals that contribute to larger corporate objectives. Furthermore, these are pursued under the umbrella of a company's core values (service, innovation). Great managers are able to develop individuals' unique talents and synergize them with the talents of others. A manager's role is comparable to the role of a football coach. They assemble a team of eleven players on the field, each with their own strength (receiving, blocking, passing, kicking). He writes plays and coaches the players through their execution. Great companies are comprised of individuals with strengths (sales, marketing, technology) all working toward common goals prescribed by leaders and managers.

Purpose Is a Labor of Love

Michael Kane—not the actor, the Beverly Hills business manager—is a friend of mine whose passion is SCUBA diving. He takes any chance he gets to steal away for a weekend, or travel to exotic locales, in search of sunken ships, lost treasures, or exploring previously unexplored caves.

We've had dinner many times, and I've watched him quickly bow out because he needs to wake up at 4 a.m. to prepare for a scuba expedition. This isn't like a trip to the beach or a weekend getaway. When he explained the planning process, it sounded more like a Navy Seal expedition.

He told me the actual scuba event involves planning several days in advance for steps like blending proper gases (oxygen) mixes. Depending on the chosen dive site, you may dive with air, nitrox or trimix, whether it's a recreational dive or a more advanced dive.

Packing includes regulators, BCD (Buoyancy Compensation Device), masks, fins, wetsuits or dry suits, computers, compasses, tanks, lights, camera, video equipment, dry suit undergarments, argon (specialized form of "air" that warms a dry suit), SPG (Submersible Pressure Gauge) and decompression gases.

Besides the equipment details, there are logistics planning. Adventuresome scuba divers must secure a reservation on a local charter boat. They arrive early in the morning on the dock and begin loading the boat for the trip. You organize your gear on the two-hour boat ride. During the day, you can do three or four dives, depending on the depth of the dives and weather conditions. You arrive back at the dock at six at night and then rinse all your equipment free of salt water—and this is an *easy* trip. When you have a clearly defined purpose that aligns with your passions, the myriad of details—however difficult—are merely stepping-stones, not stumbling-blocks.

If the trip is to an exotic location, the level of preparation increases significantly. You may need to secure permits from local governments; dive shops may not be within reasonable distances, so you need to prepare for contingencies such as broken gear and the need to fill your tanks. Most importantly, emergency evacuation plans must be considered in case a diver is injured. Not every dive site is close to the local pier; the best and most rewarding dive sites are in remote locations in undisturbed—or never-before-explored--caves and sunken ships.

For example, when he dove the South China Sea, the nearest piece of land was about 800 miles away, and helicopter evacuations in China were not easily accessible. When they ventured deep into the Akumal jungle, it took them two days to get to the dive site without communications. If someone were injured during a dive, it would have taken a minimum of two days to journey through the jungle to get the diver to a hyperbaric chamber. This is a daunting task when moving equipment through a jungle that requires mules to haul the dive gear, food supplies and camping equipment.

Lost Love of Labor

Mike is a talented SCUBA diver. Mike is a horrible golfer. If you ask him to explain the details of an easy round of golf, it sounds more involved, more time consuming, and less rewarding than SCUBA diving.

He describes golf as getting the clumsy clubs in the small trunk of the car, visiting the boring golf pro shop, an average breakfast, a trek to the range, and then one frustrating shot after another. After you finish warming up, you go to the first tee where the next party solemnly stops talking while you address the ball and goof a practice swing. Public speaking is less nerve-wracking.

After the awkward first shot off the tee--followed by a swear word—the rest of your party states the obvious with comments like, "Nice shot, you hooked it, you shanked it, anybody notice where it went? I'm in the weeds, I'm in the lake, I'm in a bunker," and "C'mon!"

"It's a frustrating day and my years of baseball don't seem to help." He grins and shrugs, "I am ready to go home at about the third hole." His aversion to golf makes recreation kindle feelings of frustration.

You should feel a gravitational pull toward your activities, not fight contrary emotions. Anybody can muscle their way through an endeavor, but few people can remain engaged over a sustained period of time unless it's a labor of love. Mike doesn't mind the extra work involved with a long distance SCUBA expedition. However, because he's not naturally drawn to the game of golf, any minor inconvenience practically stops him in his tracks. In any endeavor, if you dread the process, you will not see optimal performance, you will not stay the course, you will soon abandon the venture completely. Bamboo grows willingly, not reluctantly.

The Principle of Directed Discovery

Directed Discovery is at work when you attract people and circumstances that align with your clear purpose. Thoughts create pathways for kindred events to reveal themselves to you. It is a gift you have in your genetic code and can be used to your advantage.

As hunters and gatherers, if you needed to hunt a wild boar in order to survive, you had to know what it looked like and how to distinguish it from its natural surroundings. If you could eliminate everything in the forest that was *not* a wild boar, you could find your target and feed your family. If you didn't recognize your prey against the backdrop of the forest, you didn't eat. Those that made the connection survived and, thankfully, passed on the ability to us through the gene pool. You use this innate gift to recognize an opportunity, find important resources, or even quickly locate coupons in the newspaper for products you use.

I recently watched the movie *Bullitt*, starring Steve McQueen. You may remember the nine and a half minute, white-knuckled car chase. I wish I had the chance to see it on the big screen and not my television. The chase involved a dark green, 1968 Mustang Fastback with a 390 horsepower engine, and a "Tuxedo Black" Dodge Charger R/T 440 Magnum. The chase takes place throughout San Francisco's winding streets and through the San Bruno Mountains. The cars reached speeds of 75 to over 100 miles an hour, and the scene took three weeks to shoot.

After I watched the movie, I was astounded at the number of old Mustang Fastbacks I saw on the street. Were they always there? Was there a recent surge in their popularity? Or was it because I was so impressed with the guttural rumbling of the muscle engines in the movie, that it remained top-of-mind? Now that you have been reminded of the movie and the landmark chase scene, how many old mustangs will you see?

When I shared this manifestation of Directed Discovery with participants in a workshop, I heard some good first hand accounts of the principle at work:

> "Before we had our baby, I never noticed all the baby changing stations at malls, beaches and public restrooms. After you have a baby, you begin to notice other babies. It seems like there were more diaper commercials on television. Our neighborhood appeared to have more people pushing baby strollers. The whole world seemed filled with toys, coloring books, and sippy cups."

> "When we decided to buy a house, we noticed 'for sale' signs everywhere. It seemed like the day we decided to shop for a new home, there were more articles in the paper about what to do when buying a home; more advertisements about getting a home loan. When we drove down the street, every bus bench had a smiling real estate agent and a phone number."

> "When I decided to be a comedian, everything I saw became joke material. Every little absurd thing I did during the day was valuable. Standing in line at the bank was a two-minute bit; using the lavatory on an airplane was the start of an anecdote; sitting in the dentist's chair was even more grist for the mill. Once I decided to be a comedian, humor was everywhere."

When you discuss your goals and focus on what you can do about them each day, the resources you need for their accomplishment will reveal themselves to you. It's as if your resources are highlighted, calling out to you. The more clear you are about the people, details and steps you need to get what you want, the brighter those details shine. When you capture and implement those ideas, you progressively move in your chosen direction. And that is the subject of the next chapter . . .

Bamboo Review

- Purpose and action have the power to change the world
- Purpose trumps burnout and is life-sustaining
- Purpose affects what you see in your surrounding world

Chapter 8

The Strategic Root

Bamboo pursues growth patterns that place roots and canes in favorable environments.

Planning is like the game of Frisbee: it's not a lot of fun if you do it alone. Planning is more productive when it's a discussion-driven team effort. When you do your thinking and planning in solitude, you're limited to your own experience base; when you seek the opinion of others, your experience base increases. Fresh perspectives are valuable and inspiring.

Inspiration is a catalyst that prompts you to recognize tasks that advance your game. You drive down the street and see a billboard that triggers a thought: you decide to refinance your home, switch insurance companies, or start your novel. Inspiration creates positive emotions; planning enables you to capture the emotions on paper by converting ideas to written agendas and tasks.

Juggling details in your head is stressful and creates counterproductive emotions. You *feel* buried in details; you *feel* swamped; you *feel* your life is spinning out of control. These emotions are debilitating and self-defeating. Collective thinking and planning is the antidote to fear, worry, and anxiety. Planning through discussion creates confidence, you feel less isolated in your quest, and the necessary tools are surprisingly simple.

A recorded strategy, whether on a good ol' fashioned "to do list" or an excel spreadsheet, is your map—a navigation system that steers you to your destination. If your map is incorrect, incomplete or followed inconsistently, you waste precious time and may miss the mark. If your map aligns with your destination, and is rigorously pursued, you will arrive quickly and efficiently.

Hang it on the Wall

I'm a big fan of storyboarding and post-it notes. Anytime I plan a project such as writing content for a CD, presentation, or an article, I record the brainstormed ideas on standard-sized post-its. I scribble each idea, step or assignment on a post-it and stick it on the wall. This reveals a birds-eye view of the steps required to accomplish the project, and an easy means of re-sequencing and editing.

Animation Foundation

The Walt Disney Studios developed and popularized storyboarding in the 1930's. According to Christopher Finch in *The Art of Walt Disney,* animator Webb Smith created the idea of drawing scenes on separate sheets of paper and pinning them on a bulletin board in the story sequence. The first cartoons produced with storyboards were "The Three Little Pigs" and "Steamboat Willie"—the first cartoon featuring Mickey Mouse. Each "board" told a story, and enabled others to visualize the beginning, middle and end.

The technique soon spread to businesses that used storyboards for planning ad campaigns, presenting proposals, or when trying to persuade a committee. Illustrating and scripting ideas with the ability to prioritize and edit by simply "un-sticking" or "re-pinning" the sheets of paper to the wall was fast, convenient and effective. It enables people to "walk through" a presentation.

Storyboarding facilitates sharing and communicating with others—it's very easy to stand before a mural of ideas that maps a path. It's the quintessential means of putting people on the same page, singing off the same sheet of music--they convert the abstract to the concrete. For your purposes of mapping a new career plan or creative project, it's an ideal way to engage your coach and deepen appreciation for your mission.

What once seemed overwhelming and confusing is now linear, logical and laid out in a ready-to-implement format. This builds confidence, provides focus, and simplifies the process. I call it the pizza principle: until you cut it into edible-sized slices, it is unwieldy and awkward.

The Strategic Discussion

Dialogue with your coach/mentor/trusted advisor provides focus and stimulates ideas at a more productive clip. It's a game of one-upmanship: you being with an idea about how to network, your coach improves upon it. The first idea that surfaced was "join an online social networking site." It then evolves to include dinner parties, church functions, Toastmasters, and using various internet niches. These conversations unearth possibilities that would not otherwise have been discovered. Ideas are inspired by each other's previous ideas, and some ideas are the combination of your thoughts as a team. The whole becomes greater than the sum of the parts.

Don't edit these initial strategic brainstorming sessions. The quickest way to squelch creativity is to evaluate ideas before they are communicated or recorded. Let your creative thoughts fly around the room unencumbered by logic, sequence or judgment. The objective is to generate an exhaustive list of possibilities—keep thinking until the last kernel has popped. Once the ideas have safely made it to paper, you can begin evaluating, prioritizing and editing.

Tapping Others' Talents

Your intermediate steps may require others' expertise. That's the beauty of delegation and "outsourcing": you can fill your talent gaps with others' talents. If you can't build the website for your start-up company, you can easily find someone who is an expert at web design and enjoys the work. Distinguish between the steps you will address and those better delegated to someone with the right talents.

From here, the success of your journey is a time management endeavor. It's now about making realistic commitments you can keep, and keeping your planning device handy—software or paper—so you always have the opportunity to punch holes in your agenda.

Your coach isn't off the hook yet; planning is only the price of admission—it is necessary but not sufficient to make real progress. The fine line between ideas that languish or produce is consistent implementation. Schedule another similar meeting with your coach--this time to discuss *progress.*

This is the sticking point for most people. There is no shortage of information, only dedication. We are not rewarded for our ideas and intentions; we are rewarded for what we do. If we applied what we already know and have read, we would all be rich and thin—you must put ideas to work. Sustain your enthusiasm, inspiration and urgency long enough to see tasks through to completion and engage anyone you can to ensure you remain on your path. The flowers of tomorrow are in the seeds of today.

Your Calendar Is King

Your calendar contains the tasks and appointments that establish your root system and where it is cultivated to its full, robust potential. Stay focused on your quest by doing something every day that advances and strengthens your roots. The key to fortifying your root system is to deliberately do something each day that's directed toward establishing your foundation for significant growth. This momentum is similar to physical training: you can't accomplish much with a haphazard training routine. There is no such thing as dabbling with a diet. There are no *degrees* of commitment. You are either actively invested in your quest, or merely harboring pipedreams and ill-conceived aspirations. Identify your tasks, dedicated time for your tasks, and do your tasks.

The following are examples of those who worked every day to eventually achieve stardom.

Profiles in Bamboo Patterns

Potential is not revealed haphazardly. Potential is revealed systematically. People who achieve fame, fortune, notoriety, or leave a legacy, do so by deliberately developing their potential. They perform their tasks with the constancy of purpose as predictable as the sunrise, not through irregular fits and starts. Even when bamboo appears to be at rest, the root system is advancing daily.

Athletes, entrepreneurs, and authors follow rigorous and routine plans that steadily advance them in their chosen direction. Despite outward devil-may-care appearances, they are dedicated people who enjoy their work, and operate dutifully within the borders of structured routines.

Music

A music band that meets every day to collaborate is intense work. Sitting in a studio, delivering take after take, experimenting with different sounds and lyrics is laborious and mentally taxing. It looks like fun to lounge around in jeans and play the guitar, but not when your livelihood and reputation rides on absolute perfection

What appears to be a group of people playing and enjoying their instruments is actually the product of hundreds of hours of work, practice and rehearsal. Each band member can anticipate every drum beat, vocal and instrumental passage. This kind of ownership is the product of days and weeks of deliberate efforts, not sporadic jam sessions.

Frank Sinatra was legendary for work ethic, often referred to as "the hardest working man in Hollywood." He wasn't merely talented; he developed his talents everyday of his professional career. What we saw on stage was an hour and a half created by years of experience and hundreds of hours of conscious practice.

In the 1960's, Frank Sinatra asked Quincy Jones if they could add Johnny Mandel's new song "The Shadow of your Smile" to the repertoire of songs in a performance planned for the following night at the Sands Hotel in Las Vegas. Quincy asked, "Can you learn the lyrics by then?" Frank gave him a wink and began writing the words on a legal pad over and over again so he understood the spirit and meaning of the lyrics. Quincy Jones took a nap on the plane and we he woke, Frank had 18 pages of the lyrics written over and over again, and was still writing and humming the lines.

When they did stage rehearsals, Frank added smiles and hand gestures and it was perfect by the first night of performance. Frank Sinatra, who appeared to performing spontaneously—cocktail in hand--was a behind-the scenes perfectionist. No notes on a podium, no power points, no cheat sheets. That's what's required of any true professional who wants to make the leap from mediocrity to excellence: dedicate time every day to learn, practice and improve.

When Frank would prepare to record an album, he would disappear to his home in Palm Springs and reportedly avoid liquor, phone calls and cigarettes. He would meet with his piano player and immerse himself in his work. Once the project was behind him, he could appear on stage and deliver songs with the devil-may-care freedom that defined him.

Literature

Jack Kerouac went "on the road" for seven years with his adventuresome pals, and documented his experiences in his trusty notebook. It was the 1950's and the beginning of what Kerouac labeled "a beat generation." This era produced great poets and writers, including Michael McClure, Gregory Corso, Harold Norse, Gary Snyder, Lawrence Ferlinghetti, Allen Ginsberg, William Burroughs, Ken Kesey, and Herbert Huncke. These celebrated writers are pictured in playhouses, bookstores, and at the White Horse Tavern in New York City with cigarettes and freshly poured whiskies. Newsflash: they were working. You can't render his brand of fiction sitting in an office cubicle or working the showroom floor of a car dealership. Drugs and alcohol truncated Kerouac's productive years, but his dedication, diligence, and discipline produced eighteen novels and a dozen books of poetry. Work ethic, not outward appearances, is what accomplishes great literary feats—and any other accomplishment.

Kerouac's fanfare often fails to mention that the Bard of the Beats was constantly at work. He painstakingly worked on organization and preparation before a creative blast. He carried small pads of paper and jotted notes and rolling pages of inspiring events, especially during the seven-years of his famous road trip. His final manuscript submitted to Viking Press had many revisions and edits, including a later discovery that Kerouac began first began writing *On the Road* in his native French language. His free-flowing Bebop, Jazz-infused writings were carefully constructed, yet casually referred to as spontaneous prose.

Kerouac rented a room at the Hotel Chelsea on 23rd Street in New York City, and began diligently assembling his semi-fictionalized autobiography, *On the Road*. He soon returned to his old bedroom at his mother's house in Lowell, Massachusetts, and began his six-week assault on his typewriter until the manuscript was finished. He even avoided the interruption of feeding new sheets of paper into his typewriter by purchasing a box of continuous-feed teletype paper so his stream of consciousness would not be broken. His "spontaneous prose" was the product of focus, structure and the deliberate jazz rhythms he so enjoyed.

From athletes to authors, following and living your strategy is essential. Finding people, and creating circumstances or 'colonies" that keep fire under your feet sustains your momentum accelerates progress. These catalysts are detailed in the following chapter.

Bamboo Review

- Planning is essential in achievement, and more thorough with a partner
- Time spent planning decreases the total time required for task completion
- Planning, coupled with the right tools, accelerates results

Chapter 9

The Catalyst Root

Bamboo grows stronger and faster with healthy amounts of the right accelerators: moisture, sunlight, and rich soil

A catalyst is something that causes an important event to happen. This chapter focuses on the catalysts and motivators that begin and sustain the process of realizing your potential. Three highly-effective catalysts include

- Urgency
- Accountability
- Coaching

These three catalysts put fire under your feet and eliminate procrastination.

Urgency

When I have a weekend to run a simple errand, it can take me the entire weekend to do it. Sometimes I rationalize my way out of doing it at all. "I don't really need that light bulb" is false, and the fact that I do need it will resurface later as a nagging task on my to-do list. If I need the same light bulb within the hour, I can tackle the task without a problem. Urgency is the antidote to procrastination.

This kind of focus and attention doesn't need to happen only in response to external demands; you can create that same kind of urgency for the tasks that directly relate to getting started on a project and a more productive life. Anybody can rise to the occasion if the need is great enough. Those who are able to self-impose urgency for task achievement have mastered the art of self-discipline.

If All You Had Were Two Hours

Harry Hopkins was President Roosevelt's advisor in World War II, and gravely ill toward the end of his career. He was only capable of working a couple of hours each day, and had to muster all his strength to do so. Consequently, he eliminated all unnecessary tasks and activities and focused his precious time exclusively on critical issues. Instead of his productivity plummeting, he gained a reputation for being extremely focused and effective; Churchill referred to him as "Lord Heart of the Matter." When you separate the vital from the trivial and punch away at tasks with a sniper's focus, you can make long, productive strides.

The Accordion Principle

The Accordion Principle is a contemporary name given to Parkinson's Law. Cyril Northcote Parkinson was a British historian and author. In his essay published in *The Economist* in 1955, he stated, "work expands so as to fill the time available for its completion." His theory was originally directed at inefficiencies in administrative councils and bureaucracies. It was later applied to common tasks in a variety of contexts.

Writers often share stories of a publisher requesting a manuscript in less time than in would normally take to complete one. If finishing a manuscript takes six months, but the publisher needs it in four, writers somehow rise to the occasion. Conversely, if the manuscript can be completed in six months, but the publisher wants in nine months, the task can drag out and expand to consume the nine months. The added challenge of urgency creates the necessary focus, ambition and resourcefulness. You get more done with better results in the spirit of inspiration, not desperation.

A manager at a technology company shared how he schedules staff meetings. He noticed when he scheduled one-hour meetings, they always took at least an hour. People repeated others' comments; they "piggy-backed" unnecessarily on others' feedback and held sidebar conversations on irrelevant topics. When he reduced the meeting time to thirty minutes—the thirty minutes before lunch or the end of the day—people handled planning and participation far more efficiently. No redundancies, no excess chatter, no late arrivals. The work shrunk to meet the allotted time.

Any kind of unpleasant or difficult task—regardless of its priority—weighs on your conscience, grows in your mind, causes stress, and affects attitude and productivity. The way to overcome the tendency to allow tasks to "expand," is to consciously assess the likely or allowable timeframe for accomplishment, and then use those estimates as respected parameters for getting things done.

When tasks are time-dimensioned, we muster the means for its accomplishment. Our response to these "deadlines" can be created by an old-fashioned game of beat the clock.

Beat the Clock

Beat the clock is an old time management technique. Farmers would try to "beat the sunset" in order to finish a task in the light of day. Today, it's an easy method of pushing yourself to accomplish tasks before tasks can push you to scramble and beat a deadline. The word "deadline" implies a task will expire or "die" if it isn't completed by the time we arrived at "the end of the line." Instead of buckling down to business when facing an actual deadline, "beat the clock" compels you to buckle down and beat a self-imposed deadline with the luxury of a little buffer. It's a "constructive pressure," not a debilitating stressor.

In 1950, the game show, *Beat the Clock*, first aired and became a long-standing popular TV show. Two couples were invited from the audience and asked to complete a variety of stunts within a time limit to win cash and prizes. They did everything from stuffing balloons in a lidded trashcan without breaking them; and removing marshmallows buried in Jell-O using a spoon held in a contestant's mouth. A large clock in plain view counted down the seconds.

It was entertaining to watch because of the creativity of the stunts—often involving food or coordination and skill—and the excitement generated by the ticking clock. It wasn't a question of "could the task be performed at all;" it was a question of "could the task be performed within the *allotted time*." Similarly, the tasks we procrastinate or allow to drag on aren't intrinsically difficult; they may be tedious, unpleasant (having a difficult conversation), or unexciting. However, a time-frame superimposed on the task makes it an engaging challenge.

Something Successful This Way Comes

Twenty years ago, I met Ray Bradbury, author of *Fahrenheit 451*, *The Illustrated Man*, *Something Wicked this way Comes*, *The Martian Chronicles* and hundreds of science fiction short stories.

I spoke with him at a book signing in Los Angeles, and told him I'm an aspiring author. He earnestly encouraged me to "get a thousand words on paper every day—*every day*--even if you edit or delete most of your words, get your thousand words." That advice has been stamped in my work ethic ever since. In a broader context, research reveals that whatever your endeavor, those who practice the related skills every day with the intention to improve, eventually rise to notoriety.

At the signing, he autographed my copy of his newest book, *Zen in the Art of Writing*. In the book he details his passion for writing and explains how and why he published twenty-four books, produced several plays and even an opera. His daily quest included writing and selling short stories to simply pay his bills and to satisfy demanding publishers—constantly under a time crunch.

"I didn't know it, but I was literally writing a dime novel. In the spring of 1950, it cost me nine dollars and eighty cents in dimes to write and finish the first draft of *The Fire Man*, which later became *Fahrenheit 451* . . . I located just the place: the typing room in the basement of the library at the University of California at Los Angeles. There, in neat rows, were a score of old Remington or Underwood typewriters, which rented out at a dime a half hour. You thrust your dime in, the clock ticked madly, and you typed wildly, to finish before the half hour ran out. Thus I was twice driven; by children to leave home, and by a typewriter timing device to be a maniac at the keys. Time was indeed money. I finished the first draft in roughly nine days. At 25,000 words, it was half the novel it would eventually become."

I use a digital egg timer to help maintain my focus. If I have thirty minutes of paperwork on my desk, I set the egg timer for thirty minutes and challenge myself to get things done before the alarm sounds. I ignore the phone and work quickly and efficiently to clear my desk. This may seem more fit for children—and it works equally well for them (a race to clean their room before their favorite TV show)—yet, the results are reliable. I make great strides in productivity when I batch activities, set the clock, and then prevent them from expanding beyond its reasonable time frame. I use the same tactic trying to beat the "initial decent" announcement on an airplane to finish paperwork or the book in my briefcase.

Accountability

If you only answer to yourself, you have a pushover for a coach. When you are accountable to others, you are more likely to rise to the occasion and perform tasks that are outside of your typical, daily responsibilities. Create situations where you are committed to follow through and make good on a promise

When I plan to run a few miles before work, I often lose that enthusiasm the following morning at 5 a.m. To rise from a warm bed to pound cold concrete doesn't always appeal to me. My gift of rationale comes in handy as I consider the dangers of running through intersections, turning my ankle stepping off a curb, and the long-term, negative impact on my poor 'ol knees. This is where my snooze button gets lot attention.

I combat the tendency to flake on a worthwhile task by getting someone else involved. If I lie in bed staring at the ceiling debating whether or not the run is necessary, I'm struck by guilt when I realize my running partner may be suited up and enjoying their second cup of coffee. This feeling of accountability is enough incentive to get me out of bed; the feeling of humiliation if I don't make the scheduled run is another factor.

When I need to triumph over a barrier blocking my potential, I get others involved. If I need to learn a computer program, fill out paperwork, or put something on eBay, I seek the help of others willing to partner with me on the task. If they are generous enough to help me, I can surely be considerate enough to keep an appointment. On days I would have otherwise procrastinated, I find the energy needed tackle the task because promises trump excuses.

Coaching

A coach is someone skilled in exploring opportunities with you through questioning techniques, enabling you to discover opportunities. As I stated earlier in the Communication Root chapter, "your coach enables you to separate the wheat from the chaff, and the confidence to get started on the isolated priorities that make a difference."

People often perceive the need for a coach like the need for a tutor in grade school: special attention is required to save you from failure. Coaching isn't called into play only during remedial performance. The reality is, coaching is a key ingredient in moving the needle from good to great performance through a series of conversations. These conversations highlight strengths; they are constructive, not critical. Performance without feedback is like archery through a smokescreen.

Ironically, your coach doesn't need to know as much as you do about your trade or industry in order to be effective. There is great value in *objective perspectives*. People often experience "unconscious incompetence": they don't know what they don't know, but coaching raises awareness with ideas from a new paradigm. They enable you to avoid repeating the same mistakes, and planting the same seeds hoping to yield a different kind of crop.

Engaging a coach is a growing trend as people recognize the role and significance of feedback and collective wisdom. Plato studied under Socrates whose influence is captured in Plato's books, The *Republic*, *Crito* and *Phaedrus*. Plenty of credit goes to Phil Jackson for coaching the Chicago Bulls to an astounding 6 NBA Championships: 1991-1993 and 1996-1998. When Phil announced his decision to step down as head coach of the Bulls in June of 1998, he held the highest all-time career winning percentage (.740) among all NBA coaches. In spite of the phenomenal player talent, it's the strategy and wisdom of a coach off the court arranging the efforts and team strengths who gets the atta-boy.

Coaching is a series of discussions, not a string of intermittent hints, tips and shortcuts. The ongoing dialogue isn't a step, it's a staircase, and your coach shepherds you to the top while providing feedback. They provide the observation, you deliver the repetitions.

Some coaching results are experienced quickly, like a change in outlook; the bigger payoff *evolves*, like a change in circumstances. Nobody achieved greatness alone; they had someone to guide them and hold open doors of opportunity.

Catalysts are the wind in your sails, and especially effective when you involve another person, because people tend to honor commitments to others more than commitments to themselves. People as catalysts push, encourage, motivate, and ensure you are flourishing, not floundering. Catalysts prevent your virtues of strength, versatility and contribution from unnecessarily drifting into the future.

Even when you are making progress and succeeding, it is essential to feather your nest, get organized for the next chapter in life, and be prepared for changes, although you don't see any on the horizon. Use catalysts to inspire and prepare you to look after future opportunities and future shifts in the tide. These steps ensure resiliency and quick regeneration in the face of adversity, and that is the subject of the next chapter . . .

Bamboo Review
- Urgency is the antidote to procrastination
- The clock is a simple way to create focus and engagement
- Coaches create accountability and helpful feedback

Chapter 10

The Regeneration Root

Bamboo regenerates without replanting, and yields 20 times
more timber
than trees in one-fifth the time

The Regeneration Root ensures the previous six roots remain healthy, active and in growth mode. Bamboo is a popular, emerging resource because it's a fighter and a survivor. It's quickly reborn, highly adaptive to its environment and acclimates to extreme conditions.

Similarly, you have the conscious option of preparation and proactive behavior to buffer against predictable and unpredictable events. It's like the game of billiards: you must play the table, not the pocket, both offensively and defensively. Celebrate in your present victories, strategize your future opportunities, and ever let down your guard.

Mike Tyson was on top of the world when he fought James Buster Douglas in 1990 in Tokyo, Japan. Douglas was the 42-1 underdog, and Mike Tyson had never been knocked down before. In the tenth round, it all changed when Douglas delivered a five-punch combination that sent Tyson to the mat, losing the heavyweight title.

Whether he was unprepared, over-confident or just outmatched is not the question. The lesson is simple: anybody at any time can face circumstances that exceed their abilities or are beyond their control. Resilience and regeneration is not a gift, it is the product of conscious, mindful preparation. The business of ongoing improvement

91

is up to you. Are you a work in progress, or are you merely in maintenance mode?

In 2000, General Motors began reducing their workforce. By 2009, GM had half the number of employees they did in 2000. The trend is likely to continue through 2012. Thousands of trained and capable people found themselves eliminated from a company they were a part of for years. Those with transferrable talents could find other work. Those whose talents were specific or limited to an auto assembly line had a tougher time finding meaningful jobs, or grabbed an apron and applied at Starbucks.

When the economy or entire industries undergo dramatic change, it is the workforce that is first affected. Often, these dramatic changes come swiftly and without warning. Proactive people proceed cautiously and recognize that the safe, responsible and sensible thing to do is always play a little defense and be prepared for your next chapter.

Dramatic career and personal downturns can be avoided or mitigated by developing a contingency path. You not only have your present path, lined with current talents, values and goals, but a concurrent, alternate path lined with skills development, networking resources and other projects in your pipeline.

The days of working for a single company for thirty years until your department throws you a party and hands you a gold watch are over. We are growing and changing at breakneck speed with exponential growth. The top ten in-demand jobs in 2010 didn't exist in 2004. Those who plan their days with an eye on the future ensure they can navigate any kind of terrain they may encounter on their path. In the words of George Bernard Shaw, "the best reformers the world has ever seen are those who begin on themselves."

TQP (Total Quality People)

In the competitive world of manufacturing, stagnation is the equivalent of regression. In today's rapidly changing economy, if you're not actively developing you talents, you are dying on the vine.

Kaizen is the Japanese application of W. Edwards Deming's Total Quality Management theory. Deming (1900-1993) was a statistician, college professor, author and consultant. His theories of product design and quality were more than popular, and after World War II, the Japanese summoned his services to help improve their manufacturing and business practices. In the early nineteen-eighties, when Ford Motor Company was losing billions, they called upon Deming to kick-start their Quality Movement.

Deming is recognized for his book, *Out of the Crisis,* and for codifying his theory in his 14 Points for Management. Each point serves as a guideline and premise for improved efficiency, quality and continuous improvement. His theories are still applied today in a number of industries, and inspired the popular Six Sigma management strategy initially implemented by Motorola. Here are 3 of his 14 points:

- ➢ Create a constancy of purpose toward improvement
- ➢ Improve every process
- ➢ Initiate vigorous programs for education and improvement

Essentially, if you want a better product at the end of the assembly line, you must improve the work process *along* the assembly line. Quality materials and processes breed quality products; weaknesses in the former diminish the results of the latter. Progressive changes are made by adopting the spirit and attitude of improvement, attention to education, and opening lines of communication among management.

His theories are transferable to both production lines and people. Let's consider how the theory supports the mission of *The Bamboo Principle* with a bamboo interpretation of three tenets.

Create a constancy of purpose toward improvement

You are either steadfastly committed to improving personally and fortifying your roots, or you are merely dabbling with the idea. A lack of *constancy* is like *trying* to stay in shape or *trying* to watch what you eat—you either do or you don't. It is your responsibility to remain committed to decisions via the relationship with your coach and your use of preferred catalysts.

Improve every process

The productive and the successful seek better methods for getting things done. They are committed to making their days more efficient, effective, and stress-free. The productive and the successful read books and articles that introduce new ideas for achievement. High achievers appreciate their accomplishments, yet remain focused on how the status quo can be prepared for its next improvement. In the spirit of continuous improvement, there is always an aspect of your performance that can be improved to make you more productive and competitive. Those who continue to improve prevent personal setbacks and can quickly regenerate should they face unavoidable challenges.

Initiate vigorous programs for education and improvement

This tenet points to education as the means for bringing about positive change. Top companies don't make training available as a resource; top companies make participating in their resources for training a mandated part of the culture with rewards and recognition tied to course completion. The notion that once you have climbed several rungs of the corporate ladder, you no longer need personal development workshops is not only limiting and incorrect, it has fallen out of fashion. If a guitar isn't played for a week, it falls out of tune; similarly, unused skills—or unlearned skills—throw our professional repertoire out of tune. We feel the dissonance; others hear it and see it.

High achievers schedule time to put their talents to work and achieve specific goals—the means of which require attempts at education and improvement. They read; they cull the internet for current events, and articles of interest. *They practice*. The best at their craft focus on the cultivation, maintenance and growth of their root system.

LEXUS

I have enjoyed a strategic partnership with LEXUS for the past fifteen years. I participated in several of their efforts to improve people, products and processes and witnessed them grow from a mere contender in the luxury market, to the dominant player in quality vehicles and the car-buying experience. When LEXUS launched in 1989, they were a question mark; a few years later, they were the benchmark. Their business practices are a graceful illustration of *Kaizen*. It parallels Deming's process and echoes the spirit of continuous improvement where the work is never done because quality is a journey, not a destination.

Kaizen is still followed closely today, as it improves vehicles and introduces new technology such as Hybrid and PZEV (partial-zero emission vehicles). With an eye on strong cultural values, they remain humbly satisfied with outcomes-- acknowledging a job well done, while fixated on ways to improve the next edition. They reengineer the process, and ultimately the results. Some manufactures, by comparison, are more accepting of defects and imperfections, chalking it up to an absorbable cost of doing business. Some manufacturers learn from the mistakes revealed to them by their customers. Toyota anticipates improvements; they don't beta test a car to the consumer. Bamboo people prepare in private so their public performance is first-rate.

LEXUS had a lot to prove to the skeptics and cynics who felt that Japanese luxury was not only suspect, but an oxymoron. LEXUS built and tested an impressive 450 prototypes at $250,000 per prototype, improving each subsequent edition with the help of scores of engineers and technicians. They improved the prototypes by test-driving a total of one-million miles on a track in Japan made from the same materials as a US freeway.

LEXUS' coup de grace was applying the Kaizen philosophy not only to the car, but to the car buying experience. They identified "defects" in the process (and the anxieties people had about the shopping and buying experience), and immediately made improvements. They offered luxurious lounges, complimentary car washes for its "guests," and a loaner car program that never left its coveted customer driving an inferior rental. While the competition was content with the status quo, Toyota went searching for ways to proactively distinguish their brand, their products and their services. They were focused on making waves, not treading water.

Kaizen and Potential

If you asked a Toyota or LEXUS executive if they have accomplished the mission of Toyota's founders, they would tell you they have only scratched the surface. Toyota has tremendous potential. The internet, as magnificent as it is, has tremendous potential. Medical researchers and pharmaceuticals, thankfully, have tremendous potential. You have tremendous potential. In the words of lyricist, Carolyn Leigh, *The Best Is Yet to Come.*

Bamboo people are similarly focused, almost preoccupied, with self-improvement tactics. They don't question who they are, they question how they arrived. Winners are solution-focused, not problem-centered. Luck is often attributed to those whose biography we do not appreciate; but the road to success is paved with cultivated talents, ongoing education, and an obsessive curiosity for self-improvement tactics. Resigning to stagnation is a careless handling of power and potential, not unlike a protégé who buries his Talents, and forgoes a likely life of abundance. Complacency is nothing more than rationale for avoiding regression, conveniently misinterpreting the result as "holding down the fort" and "taking care of business." Dodging defeat is nowhere near embracing victory.

Hustle Equals Muscle

Today, your opportunities to make a name for yourself and promote your company or cause are wide open to those who make the attempt. It took radio thirty-eight years to reach an audience of 50 million; television took thirteen years to reach 50 million; the internet took four; Facebook took only two years.

How can you leverage your talents through these remarkable networking channels to fortify your root system, brace against adversity, and remain in a state of strength with robust resources so you never get caught in a position of weakness? Your talents can flourish, but only in fertile ground that's been cultivated through social networks, research and communication. Opportunities are only as good as the degree to which you are prepared to take advantage of them. The more prepared you are, the more options you have to sustain your success, stability and happiness.

The lessons taught in The bamboo Principle encourage patience, productivity and perseverance. Have no regrets: no unexplored opportunities, no unfulfilled dreams, no talents left on the table that weren't put to good use. It's not only about living a life of riches; it's about living an enriched life. Your participation in the new movement of *responsible achievement* and the principles of *The Bamboo Principle* ensure that you and all those concerned will benefit as you enjoy the virtues of Strength, Versatility and Contribution. It has its roots in the laws of cause and effect, not the enticing distractions found on the path of least resistance. There are exceptions to the rule, but they don't make sensible game plans.

Bamboo Review
- Preparation enables regeneration
- Keep an eye on developing concurrent paths that ensure versatility
- Use a breadth and depth of social networking tools that increase your number of resources

Chapter 11

The World of Exceptions

Don't follow the exceptions to the rule. When people tell me their uncle ate red meat, smoked, drank whisky, and lived a full ninety years, I am reminded that some people succeed in spite of their behavior, not because of it. It is wiser to apply the basic laws of cause and effect than gamble in hopes of beating the system.

I enjoy inspiring stories of serendipity and small miracles, but they aren't transferable game plans. Crossing your fingers isn't a strategy. Rather than focus on anomalies and exceptions to the rule, make your *work ethic* exceptional and your odds for achieving success dramatically increase. It is wiser to carry a to-do list than a rabbit's foot. Eliminate rationale that justifies the path of least resistance, relies on luck, and embraces the world of exceptions.

I have seen many people identify a personal weakness, but accept the weakness with convenient rationale. I coached a manager whose potential was hindered because he was disorganized and consistently late for appointments. He was a talented manager, but he never rose above maintenance-mode because he burned his discretionary time simply looking for things on his desk and apologizing for overlooked commitments. When he called, he usually opened with an apology for a forgotten appointment. He could complete projects on time, but not without a string of preventable crises, and last minute delegation.

I suggested a planning tool that would help eliminate self-inflicted urgencies. This notion of change-for-the-better raised a few red flags. He then headed down The Boulevard of Broken Rationale stating, "I've got a system that works pretty well. My desk is a mess, but I can find what I need," he winked. I asked where he keeps his list and his calendar. He replied, "Right here!" He removed what looked like a deck of cards from his shirt pocket: a dog-eared stack of small papers, business cards, and post-its. He glowed like a child asking, "Wanna see my baseball glove?" And for his grand finale, he said, "I've made it all these years with this system, why change?" In the professional development game, shortcuts often leave us shortchanged.

He has done well in his chosen career, but at what cost? It's not his accomplishments that concern me; it's the opportunities he's missed due to poor organizational skills. Does he work longer hours than necessary? Does he battle unnecessarily stressful days? Could he be more effective if he didn't fight one fire after the next in a sea of apologies? His resistance and rationale starve and obstruct his root system that would otherwise thrive in a world governed by the laws of cause and effect.

Chapter 12

Contribution: Your Present to the Future

These chapters have introduced you to the *roots beneath results*. These roots are the foundation upon which you can build a career, a business empire, or a more fulfilling life. If you plant and cultivate your roots, you will live the virtues of bamboo: strength, versatility and contribution. These virtues ensure sustainable success for yourself and those around you—particularly the virtue of contribution.

Generations of people have shared and expressed gratitude for bamboo, inspired by centuries of contributions made by this miracle grass. It symbolizes peace, tranquility, and strength. Bamboo teaches lessons of contribution: it is ready to render its virtues when called upon. This is your opportunity.

You will appreciate the depth and breadth of your accomplishments when you experience your power and ability to change the lives of others through various forms of contributions. Remember the gratitude felt by others when you make contributions, and the tremendous satisfaction you feel when you know you have used your experience and expertise to enrich the life of someone else—perhaps even changed a life. You can free others to advance to the next level and continue the virtuous cycle.

The spirit of contribution encompasses mindset: give where and when you can--commonly called "random acts of kindness;" and *directed contribution*: scheduled activities and opportunities to give through donations of time, money and expertise. What cause or organization will you align with to further their mission and accelerate results?

We are presently making a cultural paradigm transformation about how accessible contribution opportunities are. You no longer need to be a Carnegie or Kennedy to build libraries, but you can donate books that supply their shelves. You no longer need to send money to large foundations, but you can share your wisdom at their conferences. You no longer need to run in a marathon to raise money, but you can purchase the T-shirt that represents their cause. Small, individual deeds result in large, collective accomplishments.

There is a heightened awareness of *responsible achievement* now that there are so many pieces of humanity in disrepair. Our desire to face these challenges is now greater than our past tendencies to look the other way. People, technology and ideas are now aligned with the new direction of promoting and using talents for the greater good. When people, technology and ideas synergize, we have the power solve problems and pursue opportunities through tremendous, worldwide talent-capital.

As you finish these final words, remember: it doesn't matter how I feel, it matters what you do tomorrow based on *your* feelings. In the words of Emily Dickenson, "if you ease one life of aching, you have not lived in vain." What is your legacy? You may not be able to save all the starfish trapped on the shore, but for those you do toss back in the ocean, you have made a major difference in their lives. Use the Bamboo Development Model for your path to responsible achievement. Give without remembering, receive without forgetting, and see you at the shore.

Legacy

- Do not live namelessly, nor drift at the whim of the wind
- Stamp a deep impression the future can't rescind
- The world should know that you have lived, sure as Manhattan granite
- Press like white-hot irons, deep in the flesh of the planet
- Write it, sing it, or rhyme it, in books, lyrics or verses
- Share the painted prose of wit, scorn and curses
- Never scratch your name on a moving brook or stream
- Nor trace it in powdered sand, when the wind blows fresh and mean
- Never chip your initials, on ice in the heat of June,
- Nor plant a lily on a rock, then wait for it to bloom
- Blessed with purpose you're obliged to chance that puts you here
- To serve the world as best you can, savoring sweat and tear
- Perhaps you'll move a mountain range, or one day, have a child
- Then bend a mighty river for the creatures in the wild
- Tomorrow, rise early: eat then plan and pray
- That you can build a legacy, and you can find a way
- To show your thanks to the world, for hosting you since birth
- And return the favors graciously, with gifts of equal worth